WOULD YOU RATHER?...

Overstuffed

Over 1,500 Absolutely Absurd Dilemmas to Ponder

Justin Heimberg

Published by Seven Footer Press
276 Fifth Avenue
Suite 301
New York, NY 10001

First Printing, October 2008
10 9 8 7 6 5 4 3 2
© Copyright Justin Heimberg and David Gomberg, 2008
All Rights Reserved .

Design by Tom Schirtz

ISBN-13 978-1-934734-04-9

www.wouldyourather.com / www.falls-media.com

Table of Contents

How to Use This Book

Sit around with a bunch of friends and read a question out loud. Discuss the advantages and drawbacks of each option before making a choice. Stretch, twist, and otherwise abuse your imagination to think of the multitude of ways the choice could affect you. The question is a merely a springboard for your conversation.

Everybody must choose. As the Deity proclaims, YOU MUST CHOOSE! Once everyone has chosen, move on to the next question. It's that simple.

If you receive a question directed at females, and you are a male (or vice-versa), you can do one of several things: a) move on to another question, b) answer the question anyway, or c) freak out.

On occasion, we have provided some "things to consider" when making your decisions, but do not restrict yourself to those subjects when debating. There are no limits with this book, so go ahead and binge on the inappropriate and ridiculous, overindulge on the smorgasbord of absurdity, and stuff yourself silly.

Chapter One

Deformities, Disorders, and Inconveniences (aka Curses)

These are the circumstances. An all-too familiar Deity descends from on high and informs you that, for reasons beyond your understanding, you must live the remainder of your life plagued with a terrible curse—an outrageous physical deformity, a bizarre behavioral disorder, an irksome inconvenience, etc. You need not feel entirely powerless, however. He allows you to choose between two possible fates.

Would you rather...

have Parmesan cheese dandruff

OR

bubble wrap acne?

Would you rather...

sneeze out of your ass

OR

fart out of your nose?

Would you rather have your child's high school guidance counselor be...

Paula Abdul *OR* Simon Cowell?

Donald Trump *OR* the hosts from *What Not To Wear*?

Charles Manson *OR* Q*bert?

Would you rather...

walk like a runway fashion model all the time

OR

automatically revert to jazz hands whenever your hands are not in use?

YOU MUST CHOOSE!

Would you rather...

be compelled to enter every room by jumping into the doorway with an imaginary pistol drawn like the star of a '70s cop show

OR

invariably make your orgasm face instead of smiling when being photographed?

Would you rather be a Siamese twin...

connected at the soles of your feet *OR* at the lips?

by the fingertips *OR* by the hair?

at the buttocks *OR* at the elbows/knees?

your feet on your twin's shoulders *OR* his/her feet on yours?

with Scott Baio *OR* Hulk Hogan?

Would you rather...

be limited to N.W.A. tunes when playing goodnight lullabies to your children

OR

be limited to listening to Barney songs when in the car?

Would you rather...

have an indelible grape Kool-Aid mustache

OR

have permanent Doritos residue on your fingertips?

YOU MUST CHOOSE!

Would you rather...

make the sounds of the Bionic Man when straining physically

OR

make the sound of the *Jeopardy* theme when straining mentally?

Things to consider: test-taking, gym class

Would you rather...

have a speech impediment where you switch "f" sounds and "d" sounds

OR

where you switch "c" sounds and "r" sounds?

Things to consider: the runt of the litter, rock-hard abs, reading *The Ugly Duckling*

Would you rather...

compulsively shadow-box in your sleep

OR

have a penis which, upon getting an erection, points to the correct time like the hour hand on a clock?

Things to consider: sleeping next to someone, breaking nightstand lamps, 3:30

YOU MUST CHOOSE!

Hostage Crisis

These are the circumstances: You have been taken hostage by a group of militant terrorists. (They work for the Deity.) The terrorists' leader says he will allow the U.S. government to send one person in to negotiate your fate.

Would you rather your hostage negotiator be...

Dick Vitale *OR* Ike Turner?

Jimmy Carter *OR* Pamela Anderson?

Terry Bradshaw *OR* a mime?

Would you rather...

have an 8-inch wide innie belly button

OR

have a 10-inch long outie belly button?

Would you rather...

have a horizontal butt crack

OR

vertically aligned breasts?

YOU MUST CHOOSE!

Would you rather have a tattoo of...

various geometric formulas **OR** all the U.S. vice presidents' heads?

the faces of Bartles and Jaymes on each butt cheek **OR** a gang style tattoo of "N I M O Y" across your chest?

a scratch-and-sniff tattoo of a pickle **OR** a tattoo consisting of the Chinese character for "trite"?

a tattoo across your back of Voltaire struggling to perform auto-fellatio **OR** an ass crack extension tattoo?

Would you rather...

appear as Wolf Blitzer in the mirror

OR

have the voice in your head sound like Tommy Chong?

Would you rather...

have mood lips (change color according to your mood)

OR

make the sound of the shaking of Boggle letter cubes when laughing?

YOU MUST CHOOSE!

Would you rather...

have your eyes always moving as if watching a ping-pong match

OR

speak in the voice, volume, and intensity of a screaming Janis Joplin when speaking to anyone under 7 years old?

Would you rather...

have a written lisp

OR

fizz up like Alkaseltzer when in the water?
Things to consider: thwimming

Would you rather...

have anti-gravity hair

OR

have all your dreams written and directed by those guys who made those blaxploitation films of the '70s?

Would you rather...

be 50 pounds heavier and look it

OR

300 pounds heavier but look the same as you do now?

YOU MUST CHOOSE!

Would you rather...

HAVE FINGERNAILS THAT GROW AT THE RATE OF ONE INCH PER MINUTE

OR

HAVE PUBIC HAIR THAT GROWS AT THE SAME RATE?

Would you rather...

have Twizzlers for hair

OR

Sharpie markers for fingers?
Things to consider: irresistible tendency to smell your fingers, ravenous coworkers, scratching your back

Would you rather...

have a comb-over from your eyebrows

OR

from your back hair?

Would you rather...

speak in the rhythm of the *The A-Team* theme song

OR

blink to the tune of "Whoomp, There It Is"?

Would you rather...

have to name your kids after Starbucks sizes

OR

after famous robots?
Things to consider: What if your Venti grows bigger than your Grande?, R2-D2, Seven of Nine, Twiki

YOU MUST CHOOSE!

Would you rather...
be compelled to sign off every phone conversation with "Ain't no thang"

OR

invariably tag on a my "My Liege" at the end of all your sentences?

Would you rather...
have permanently lathered hair

OR

only be able to move around by moon-walking?

Would you rather...
vomit Super Balls

OR

urinate Crazy String?

Would you rather have your cell phone ring function set on...
First Degree Burn *OR* Vietnam War Flashback?

Ooze *OR* Lemon?

Wet Hacking Cough *OR* Surly Frenchman?

YOU MUST CHOOSE!

Would you rather...

have your ears and nipples switch places

OR

your nose and genitals?
Things to consider: cutting ear holes in sweaters, foreplay

Would you rather...

have Pamela Anderson's body from the waist up and Rosie O'Donnell's from the waist down

OR

Rosie O'Donnell's from the waist up and Pamela Anderson's from the waist down?
Things to consider: TV anchor career, toppling

Would you rather...

have lit candle wicks for hair *OR* asparagus for fingers?

worms for eyelashes *OR* corduroy skin?

a pair of fuzzy dice for tonsils *OR* Ralph Lauren Polo logos for nipples?

Would you rather...

have glow-in-the-dark veins

OR

have veins that bulge out a half-inch from your body?

YOU MUST CHOOSE!

14

CRY HOT TAR

SNEEZE WITH THE FORCE
OF A DOUBLE BARREL
SHOTGUN?

Would you rather...

HAVE YOUR CELL PHONE RING FUNCTION SET ON "AIRHORN"

OR

"TASER"?

Would you rather...

snore the sound of a dial-up modem

OR

fart the sound of a rapid-fire machine gun?

Would you rather...

have 14 navels *OR* 24 toes?

6 lips *OR* 34 fingers?

1 nostril *OR* 8 nostrils?

15 fingers *OR* 3 tongues?

no nipples *OR* 11 nipples?
Things to consider: Reread now as "**Would you rather date someone who had...**"

Would you rather...

everything you say be considered an insult

OR

a come-on?

Would you rather...

see in Xbox graphic quality

OR

see in strobe light?

YOU MUST CHOOSE!

Would you rather...

HAVE LIVING EYEBROWS THAT CRAWL ABOUT YOUR FACE

OR

SKIN THAT DOESN'T TAN UPON DIRECT CONTACT WITH SUNLIGHT, BUT RATHER PLAIDS?

Would you rather...

have a comic-book-style thought bubble

OR

a comic-book-style dialogue bubble?

Things to consider: loss of privacy, hiding your thoughts with a big hat, ability to converse with the deaf, inability to converse with the blind

Would you rather...

have an intense urge to whisper sweet nothings into the ears of bus drivers as you pay your fare

OR

have parents who affectionately refer to you as "anal cakes"?

Things to consider: teacher-parent conferences, wedding toasts

Would you rather always have to wear...

pants four sizes too small *OR* 10-inch high heels?

a tight tube top that says "bad girl" *OR* used teabag earrings?

NFL referee garb *OR* a wizard's robe and hat?

Would you rather...

have a website stream live video of all your showers

OR

all your bowel movements?

YOU MUST CHOOSE!

Would you rather be stuck on a desert island with...

Jack from *Lost* (Matthew Fox) *OR* Sawyer (Josh Holloway)?

daily delivery of the *New York Times* Comics section *OR* the Obituaries section?

a thesaurus *OR* a copy of a *Plumpers* porn magazine?
How about a publication that combines both features?

Would you rather...

have a nose that pulsates like a human heart

OR

be allowed to use only toothpaste for all hygiene purposes/processes?

Would you rather...

have a rare disorder that allows you to dispose of bodily waste only in pool table pockets

OR

ever so slowly morph into Bob Barker as you age?

YOU MUST CHOOSE!

Would you rather...

LIVE IN A HOUSE DESIGNED BY M.C. ESCHER

OR

MC HAMMER?

Interior Motives

The Deity is into anti-Feng Shui, the ancient Japanese art of the disharmonious placement and arrangement of objects in a given space. With this in mind, he decides your home needs some shaping up.

Would you rather...

have American cheese linens

OR

wall-to-wall ground-beef carpet?

Would you rather...

have *Prince Valiant* comic strip wallpaper

OR

Willis Reed permanently residing on your loveseat?

YOU MUST CHOOSE!

Would you rather...

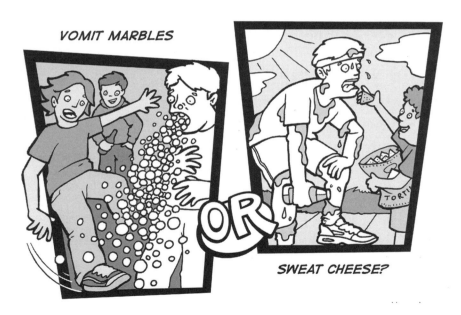

VOMIT MARBLES

OR

SWEAT CHEESE?

Would you rather... vomit marbles *OR* sweat cheese?

Pro Vomit Marbles—Justin Heimberg

When you sweat cheese, remember we're talking about your whole body: under your arms, inner thighs, every nook and cranny. Every orifice. Imagine the cheese build-up in your crack on a hot day—that is serious swamp ass. You'd end up with anal hair dreads (ahd's). Cheese sweat would also wreak havoc on your sex life. You're getting hot and heavy and you start to exude a little pepperjack. Vomiting marbles would be a little painful, sure, but what catharsis isn't? And imagine how cool the sound of the marbles hitting the floor would be. And then you've got something to do to kill time: a nice game of gastric juice-covered marbles. In fact, if harnessed right, projectile marble vomit is a self-defense weapon; it's like having a can of mace at all times.

Pro Cheese—David Gomberg

Sweating cheese is a good thing. You'd never have to buy food again. Anytime you are hungry, just build up a sweat. Maybe you even carry some crackers in your pocket (like you don't already!). As for your sex life, nothing wrong with spicing things up by bringing a little food play into your foreplay. In any case, vomiting marbles is agony. Throwing up liquid is bad enough. Imagine a bunch of hard spheres being violently summoned from your stomach up through your throat and out your mouth, beating up your uvula like a boxing speed bag.

YOU MUST CHOOSE!

25

Chapter Two

SEX

Like the deities and demigods of the Greeks, this is a god concerned with the earthly delights of hedonism. Perhaps *concerned* is not a strong enough word. Obsessed. Morbidly. Particularly in the comings and goings of his pet mortals. And so for these reasons, and others beyond your understanding, he feels that your sex life could be so much more interesting.

Would you rather...

never experience orgasm

OR

perpetually experience orgasm?

Things to consider: business meetings, funerals, public speaking

Would you rather have sex with...

Leonardo Dicaprio *OR* Russell Crowe?

George Clooney *OR* John Goodman if they exchanged weights?

Dick Cheney *OR* the Burger King mascot?

old James Bond (Sean Connery in his prime) *OR* new James Bond (Daniel Craig)?

a soft and tender Tony Danza *OR* a fast and furious Mr. Belvedere?

Would you rather have sex with...

Charlize Theron *OR* Lucy Liu?

Mandy Moore *OR* Jaime Pressly?

Natalie Portman *OR* Jennifer Lopez if they had each other's butts?

an unenthusiastic Ashlee Simpson *OR* a down-and-dirty Nancy Pelosi?

classy Christina Aguilera *OR* slutty Christina Aguilera?

YOU MUST CHOOSE!

SEX

Would you rather... *(Men: Read as "...have a partner with...")*

have breast implants made of Nerf **OR** Play-Doh?

quarters **OR** coffee grounds?

helium **OR** Pillsbury Doughboys?

Would you rather...

have your genitalia located on the top of your head

OR

the bottom of your left foot?
Things to consider: jogging, hats, the sexual act, masturbation

Would you rather...

have a permanent smile
OR
a permanent erection?
Things to consider: church, visiting grandma, funerals

Would you rather...

have to use condoms two times too big **OR** two times too small?

aluminum foil condoms **OR** the same condom over and over?

condoms covered in sandpaper **OR** condoms covered
with pictures of your mother?

YOU MUST CHOOSE!

Word Problems

You have to marry someone whose weight is twice their IQ if they are a woman and three times their IQ if they are a man? They are of average height (and not all muscle). **What IQ do you choose?**

Repeat the question above with the weight being 1.5 times the IQ for women and two times the IQ for men.

(Women) You have to sex with a man whose penis is 1/10 of his age (in inches). **What age man do you choose?**

(Men) You get to have sex with someone whose breast size measurement is half their age? **What age do you choose?** (Cup size is proportional and breasts are firm.)

Would you rather...

have to use sign language to talk dirty

OR

have to use clinical terms to talk dirty? (for example, "Penetrate that vagina!"; "Lick that mons pubis!"; "Ram that glans against the epidermis of the vulva!")

Would you rather have sex with...

just the top half of Jessica Alba

OR

just the bottom half of Jessica Alba?

YOU MUST CHOOSE!

Would you rather...

HAVE COMMERCIAL INTERRUPTIONS DURING MASTURBATION FANTASIES

OR

HAVE TO MASTURBATE WITH THE MANDATORY USE OF A SESAME STREET'S ELMO HAND PUPPET?

Would you rather...

have pubic hair in the style of Princess Leia's hair *OR* ZZ Top-beard style?

have steel wool pubes *OR* Velcro pubic hair?

have ingrown pubic hair *OR* pubes that grow up and around your body like ivy on a house?

Things to consider: Other works that have dedicated an entire quarter page to pubic hair—*Hamlet, Rapunzel 2: The Revenge*, the Articles of Confederation, *Where's Waldo?*, *Band of Brothers*

Would you rather your only porn be...

six-second clips of hot people *OR* two-minute clips of moderately attractive people?

verbose, subtle erotic fiction *OR* pornographic Magic Eye 3D pictures (the ones where you have to stare just right until the image comes into focus)?

Renaissance art *OR* the National Geographic specials about indigenous tribes?

Would you rather...

speak in the voice and style of Jar Jar Binks during sex

OR

have blurred, pixilated privates like they use to censor nudity on TV?

Things to consider: benefits of blurring if you are a poorly endowed man

YOU MUST CHOOSE!

Would you rather...

have a lover who is 6'4" with 32A breasts

OR

4'5" with 42EEE breasts?

Would you rather...

ejaculate grape soda

OR

ejaculate a small coiled novelty snake akin to those found in April Fool's peanut brittle jars?

Would you rather have phone sex with...

Chris Matthews *OR* Flavor Flav?

William Faulkner *OR* Kermit the Frog?

Nelson Mandela and Posh Spice (on conference) *OR* Anna Kournikova and Squiggy from *Laverne & Shirley*?

YOU MUST CHOOSE!

Would you rather have phone sex with...

Celine Dion *OR* Maya Angelou?

Hillary Clinton *OR* Nancy Grace?

a severely congested Alyssa Milano *OR* Katie Couric?

Would you rather...

have Angelina Jolie as your personal sex slave *OR* an unlimited supply of pork? Jolie as your sex slave *OR* unlimited pork and season tickets to all sporting events? Jolie as your sex slave *OR* the pork, season tickets, and a personal minstrel who records your deeds in song?

Would you rather...

have joy buzzers built into your breasts

OR

have your G-spot located under your right armpit? In your left nostril? In the lunch box of a fifth-grader in Milwaukee?

YOU MUST CHOOSE!

Would you rather...

eliminate PDA's (as in "public displays of affection")

OR

eliminate PDA's (as in people using "personal digital assistants" when in public)?

Would you rather...

(Women: Read as "... have a partner who has...")
have a penis that can change circumference

OR

that can change length?

Would you rather...

have sex with all celebrities with last names that begin with "L" *OR* "B"?

"G" *OR* "R"?

"Smi..." *OR* "Cyru..."?

Would you rather...

have to masturbate wearing a condom

OR

have to masturbate to sex symbols pre-1979?

YOU MUST CHOOSE!

The Price of Sex:
The "Add up to 100" Rule

(women) **Would you...** have sex with a 70-year-old Marlon Brando to have sex with a 30-year-old Marlon Brando? What two ages that add up to 100 would you choose?

(men) **Would you...** have sex with a future 75-year-old Jessica Alba to have sex with a 25-year-old Jessica Alba? 60/40? 82/18? Which two ages that add up to 100 would you choose?

Would you... have sex with any 70-year-old of your choice to have sex with any 30-year-old of your choice? Who would you choose for each?

Would you rather...

have sex with someone with the body of Pamela Anderson, the face of Queen Elizabeth, and the feet of Yao Ming

OR

the face of Angelina Jolie, the body of Rosie O'Donnell, and the hair of Jimmie Johnson?

YOU MUST CHOOSE!

Would you rather...

have genitalia that reduces in size 2% each time it is used

OR

genitalia that increases in size 25% each time it is used?

Would you rather...

have a scrotum that puffs up like a car airbag whenever you get scared (breasts for women)

OR

a beat-boxing anus?

Would you rather...

have a TiVo that displays information and the exact timing regarding the occurrence and quality of nudity and sex for all shows

OR

have a Microsoft Help Icon that talks dirty to you?

Things to consider: paper clip fetishes, market as "the TiVo Masturbation Guide" (patent pending)

YOU MUST CHOOSE!

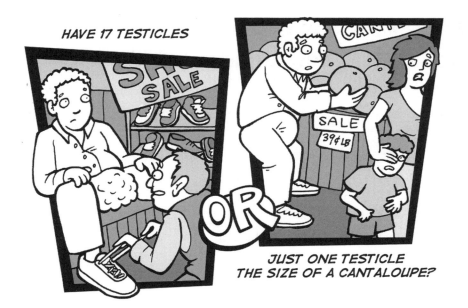

Date, Marry, Screw?

Borat, Ali G, Bruno

Pauly Shore, John Kerry, Jeffrey Dahmer

Nicole Richie, Tara Reid, Paris Hilton

Randy Jackson, Paula Abdul, Simon Cowell

Drunk Lindsay Lohan, sober Lindsay Lohan, strung-out Lindsay Lohan

Date, Marry, Screw, Head-butt, Reenact a Civil War Battle Against, or Eat Pork With?

Matthew Perry, Emeril Lagasse, Steve Buscemi, Latrell Sprewell, Justin Timberlake

Sarah Silverman, Sharon Osborne, Sally Jessy Raphael, Joan of Arc, Ann Coulter, Mia Hamm

David Copperfield, Mark Wahlberg, Tony Little, Steven Segal, Gomberg, *Sesame Street's* Count von Count

Would you rather...

have a cell phone that is also an MP3 player and a camera

OR

that is also a boomerang and a vibrator?

YOU MUST CHOOSE!

45

Would you rather...

have "buffering" to your masturbation fantasies like a slow streaming video on the Web

OR

have any dialogue in your masturbation fantasies spoken in Korean?

Would you rather...

have a three-way with TomKat (Tom Cruise and Katie Holmes) *OR* Brangelina (Brad Pitt and Angelina Jolie)?

the old Beniffer (Ben Affleck and J-Lo) *OR* the new Bennifer (Ben Affleck and Jennifer Garner)?

BobCat (Bob Saget and Catherine Zeta Jones) *OR* Phillary (Dr. Phil and Hillary Duff)?

Dobberts (Lou Dobbs and Julia Roberts) *OR* BoutrosBoutrosHalle (Boutros Boutros-Ghali and Halle Berry)?

YOU MUST CHOOSE!

Would you rather have...

(Women: Read the following questions as "...have a partner with...")

a 4-inch penis with a 2-inch diameter **OR** an 8-inch penis with a half-inch diameter?

an 8-inch penis that was always soft **OR** a 3-inch penis that was always hard?

a retractable penis **OR** a detachable penis?

a penis able to drink like an elephant uses his trunk **OR** a penis that glows in the dark when you twist the head?

SEX

YOU MUST CHOOSE!

Would you rather...

Would you rather...

orgasm once every 20 years *OR* once every 20 seconds?

20 Years—Justin Heimberg

If you orgasm ever 20 seconds, you simply cannot function in life. Imagine that PowerPoint presentation at work. Your wedding day. Your wedding night. Funerals. Parenting. And don't say you'd get used to it and be able to muffle your ecstasy. If that were the case, we'd all be used to it by now. After our first dozen or so, we'd orgasm with humdrum nods of approval without a varied breath, not cross-eyed facial pandemonium coupled with sounds we are otherwise incapable of. You never get used to an orgasm. That's why we need more. Almost constant orgasm would cast you out of society, and there you would stay, lying in a gutter somewhere in a pool of your own goods, the happiest bum in the world.

20 Seconds—David Gomberg

Buy me some specially lined pants, because there is no way you can go through life orgasming every 20 years. This goes beyond being a bit cranky. You'd go crazy. You'd murder. Steal. You'd write a horrible off-Broadway play. And in a sense, yes, the orgasms you actually have will be intense, perhaps producing enough ejaculate to power a small exurb; but when, where, and why will they come? That's real pressure to get that moment right. For men, if you are looking to reproduce, you'd need to can that sucker in a golden urn and protect it like a holy seminal shroud. Take the mess. It's worth it. No worse than a runny nose. It's just like having a cold of the crotch.

YOU MUST CHOOSE!

49

Chapter Three

Fashion and Style

There are deities who are oblivious to the ebb and flow of style. Powerful gods tend to be more concerned with the evolution of their world's humanity than that of hemlines and hairstyles. But this is not your daddy's deity (i.e., Jesus). This is a far more metrosexual deity. It's time for a makeover, Deity-style.

Would you rather...

have to wear clothes five sizes too small

OR

have to wear articles of clothing on a different part of the body than they were intended for?

Things to consider: pants for shirt, socks for gloves, hat for pants, underwear for ascot

Would you rather...

have to keep your keys permanently attached to a hoop earring

OR

have to always wear your socks on the outside of your shoes?

Would you rather always have to wear...

traditional Samurai garb *OR* a matador outfit?

a 20-pound top hat *OR* cross-country skis?

a suit of armor *OR* clothes made from Saran Wrap?

cozy feet-encasing pajamas *OR* a blazer featuring Postmaster Generals from history?

YOU MUST CHOOSE!

Would you rather...

HAVE A VELCRO BEARD

OR

AN AFRO OF CRAZY STRAWS?

For 370,000 tax-free dollars, would

you... for the rest of your life, wear a piano tie for all formal occasions including business meetings, weddings, and funerals?

Would you... wear a T-shirt that said "Certified Muff Diver" to the

office on Casual Friday for $22,000? What about semi-transparent white slacks under which you have briefs emblazoned with "The Fartbeat of America"?

What is the most ridiculous thing you'd wear to the office for a day for $5,000?

For $25,000, while attending a family reunion, **would you** wear cutoff Daisy Duke jean shorts with an inch-diameter crotch seam? What are the shortest cutoff jeans you'd wear for $25,000 as measured by crotch diameter?

Would you rather...

have to wear all of your clothing inside out

OR

have to use an immortal flounder for a wallet?

Things to consider: important business lunches where you pick up the check, dropping your fish, "Immortal Flounder" = good band name

YOU MUST CHOOSE!

Would you rather always have to wear...

clothes in the style of an 8-year-old *OR* an 80-year-old?

a full Georgetown Hoya uniform *OR* an eye patch?

pleather *OR* highly fashionable outfits except that the shirts all have holes cut out at the nipples?

Would you rather...

be judged by *Project Runway's* fashion judges as you leave for work each day

OR

have all your meals critiqued by *Top Chef* judges?
Things to consider: Michael Kors = Fat Anthony Michael Hall; Tom Colicchio = Fat Cal Ripken, Jr. (Google them.)

Would you rather...

have a nose piercing with a chain connected to a sparrow

OR

have a massive one hair comb-over that winds back and forth on your head?

Would you rather...

have asymmetrical breast implants

OR

have two equal-size breast implants...on your knees?

YOU MUST CHOOSE!

Would you rather...

HAVE EARRINGS THAT WORK AS BLUETOOTH HEADSETS

OR

A TONGUE PIERCING THAT WORKS AS A BREATH MINT?

Would you rather...

always have to wear ultra-ultra low-riding jeans (waistline is barely above the genitals and well below the pubic line)

OR

ultra-high riding jeans (waistline is above the nipples)?

Go Low!—Justin Heimberg

The lower the waistline, the better as far as I'm concerned. I'm not afraid of showing a little tuft. In fact, let's go right ahead and market them as "Tuft Jeans." Write the brand name in yellow stitching and a scraggly font that looks like pubic hair and everything. Slogan: "Just Enough Tuft." And on the flip side, having a little a-crack exposed isn't a bad idea either. It's a place to rest your cigarette. On the contrary, denim up to and around the nipples is like being in a straitjacket or worse, a unitard. You'd look like a merman. And imagine the nipple burn.

No Low!—David Gomberg

First of all, you do not want to see Heimberg's tuft. It's like staring at Medusa; you turn to stone. So just imagine the parade of pubic shrubbery one would be sentenced to see if Tuft Jeans hit the mass market. High-cinched jeans may limit mobility but they also act as a girdle, giving a slimming effect. It's really just overalls without the straps. Granted they're super-tight overalls with a belt across the nipples, but who hasn't taken a belt across the nipples at some point, right?... Anyone?

YOU MUST CHOOSE!

Chapter Four

Immoral Dilemmas

Since the beginning of eternity, the Deity has always been fascinated by humankind's capacity for right and wrong. He impishly delights in the vicarious struggles of conscience ping-ponging during a mortal's decision making process. And so he poses to you these questions of conscience.

An unbelievably attractive spouse of a close friend offers you the chance for a one-time "no one will know" affair. Do you partake in oral or anal sex?

You are walking down the street when you see someone drop a $100 bill and walk off obliviously. Do you spend the money on meth or crack?

You hear a woman screaming as if being attacked in the parking lot behind your apartment building. Do you watch *The Office* or *CSI*?

You're attractive, but poor and without skills. Someone offers you a lot of money to work for an escort service. How can I get in touch with you?

The teacher asks if you wrote your son's book report. Your son claimed he did it, but the teacher's right. Do you concentrate on defending the report's racism or anti-Semitism?

You're buying a house from an old lady. She's asking a price that is way too low. Do you partake in oral or anal sex?

Paper or plastic?

A social agency wants to establish a residence for seven retarded adults next door to your house. Another neighbor has written up a petition against the home and asks you to sign. Do you dominate the retards in basketball or football?

Your father is having an affair and your mother is unaware of it. High five or fist bump?

YOU MUST CHOOSE!

Venti or grande?

It's Thursday, and you are raping an antelope. Do you wear a Nixon mask?

You remarry and find that your new spouse is allergic to the dog you've had for eight years. Who do you put down first?

It's 4am and you are stopped at a red light on a country road that seems like it's never going to change. No one is in sight. Do you masturbate with your left or right hand?

Democrat or Republican?

You're in your hometown and you bump into your old girlfriend. With your penis. Over and over. Such is life.

You've ensnared the nation in a five-year war based on faulty intelligence, you've broken the military, and helped precipitate the nation's worst economic crisis since the depression. Tax breaks for the rich or tax breaks for the rich?

During one of your weekly rendezvous, a prostitute gives you a choice between oral and anal sex. When you publicly renounce your governorship, do you force your wife to stand by your side?

YOU MUST CHOOSE!

Chapter Five

What's Your Price?
Part 1

These are the circumstances: A powerful deity descends from on high, and for reasons beyond your understanding informs you that you are about to face temptation. You will be presented with an opportunity that will test the boundaries of your conscience, measure your threshold for pain, or in some other fashion, determine the true nature of your character. Only you know the truth. Only you can decide if the money is worth it. Only you can answer... What's Your Price?

All in the Family

Would you... wearing a mask, punch your grandmother as hard as you can in the back of the neck once for $10,000 if she never found out it was you? Would you do it for $100,000? $1,000,000?

What is the hardest you would punch her for $100,000? Demonstrate.

Would you... give two intense hickeys to your grandfather for $2,000? Would it kill him?

Would you... make out with your sibling for two minutes for $5,000? One minute? 30 seconds? What would be your lowest dollar-per-second rate?

Would you... never communicate with your mother again for $1,000,000? What if you could communicate with her but only in freestyle rap?

WHAT'S YOUR PRICE!?

The Price of Pain

Would you... cheese-grate the skin off your knees for $15,000? $50,000? $300,000? What's your price?

Would you... iron your clothes while wearing them for $25,000?

Would you... put 1,000 staples into your body anywhere you like for $145,000? How about only 50 staples placed wherever a heartless torturer chooses?
Things to consider: Would you then remove them?

Would you... have you entire body waxed with duct tape for $10,000?

Would you... clip your tonsils with garden clippers for $750,000?

WHAT'S YOUR PRICE!?

Sex Education

Would you... have sex with a manatee to have sex with all of last year's *Playboy* Playmates (men); with 10 Hollywood leading men of your choice (women)?

Would you... have sex with ten 1's to have sex with one 10? Would you have sex with five 2's to have sex with one 10? Siamese twin 5's to have sex with a 10?

How much would you... pay to have sex with Angelina Jolie (men)/Brad Pitt (women) for one night? What if he/she was suffering from herpes? A severe bout of dysentery? Tourette's Syndrome?

Would you... have sex with Halle Berry (men)/Tom Brady (women) if it made you speak with a lisp for the rest of your life?

$ **WHAT'S YOUR PRICE!?** $

You're a Poser

Would you... pose in *Playboy/Playgirl* for $250,000? *Penthouse?*
Hustler? Best of Bukkake? Golden Shower Monthly?

Which of the following would you pose in for $700,000?

Juggs?

Swank?

Plumpers?

Barely Legal?

Barely Ambulatory?

Sexual Deviant Biweekly?

Bisexual Deviant Weekly?

Bowling Wrist-Brace Fetish Monthly?

What is the most provocative publication you'd pose in for $100,000?

WHAT'S YOUR PRICE!?

Indigestion Question

Would you... scarf down the contents of a bug-zapper bag for $4,500? What if you could blend it up first?

Would you... tongue clean the urinals at your favorite sports team's arena for season tickets? How about to be on the team for a game?

Would you... eat a chicken breast generously encrusted in pubic hair for $26,000? Does it in any way depend on whose pubic hair it is?

Would you... eat the "X" volume of the encyclopedia if you would remember it exactly? Which books/pages would you eat if eating them ingrained their contents perfectly in your memory?

WHAT'S YOUR PRICE!?

Fast Money

Would you... sleep with your significant other's mom for $250,000 if you never got caught?

Would you... spend two months wearing a mullet for $2,000? Would there be any ramifications?

Would you... gain 150 pounds for $30,000? Like meat at the supermarket, how many dollars per pound would you charge, and what is the max you would gain?

Would you... floss with a recently removed tapeworm for $10,000?

Would you... eat a bologna-sized slice of human flesh for $1,000? $50,000? $1,000,000?

WHAT'S YOUR PRICE!?

Conscience Crushers

The Deity wants to find out who you truly are. "I'm a good person," you claim. But are you really?

Would you... write anonymous hate mail to 10 orphans saying that they will never be adopted and that no one loves them for $800,000? $500,000? $100,000? How low would you go?

Would you... run over a litter of stray kittens with a lawnmower for $75,000? $250,000? $2,000,000? What's your price?

Would you... "accidentally" bump into a 4-year-old at a playground, knocking him over for $800?

WHAT'S YOUR PRICE!?

Masturbance

Would you... masturbate with your off hand for the rest of your life for $45,000?

Would you... masturbate with a condom on for the rest of your life for $100,000?

Would you... masturbate with "When the Saints Come Marching In" playing loudly in the background for the rest of your life for $300,000?

Would you... masturbate to only *Good Housekeeping* magazine for the rest of your life for $175,000? *New Yorker* cartoons? Model airplane instructions? What one nonpornographic publication would you choose if you could choose only one?

WHAT'S YOUR PRICE!?

Thinkers

Would you... invent a machine that accelerated all technological advances but directly caused thousands of deaths a year?
Things to consider: Would you invent the car?

Would you... invent a machine that created amazingly delicious sauces but caused 1,000 hand injuries a year and killed one extremely dumb person?
Things to consider: Would you invent the blender?

Would you... invent a machine that worsened the hair of thousands of ignorant people and killed one unbelievably stupid and perverted person?
Things to consider: Would you invent the Crimper?

WHAT'S YOUR PRICE!?

Fun in the Sun

Would you... go on the beach in a string thong and Tevas for the whole afternoon for $900?

Would you... bury your body in the sand with just your head protruding for three hours for $3,000? Same thing with just your balls protruding (you have a breathing tube)?

Would you rather... spend a 90 degree day at the beach in a string thong or a wool sweater and ski pants?

Would you... tan half of your body by wearing a special suit for a week at the beach for $500? What strange tan line would you do for $500? Farmer's tan? Inverse farmer's tan?

WHAT'S YOUR PRICE!?

Bath Time

Would you... bathe daily in a tub of au jus for $500,000? Which fluids would you bathe in daily for $500,000 deposited directly into your bank account? Answer "yes" or "no" to the following:

Nacho cheese?

Creamed spinach?

Saliva, your own?

Saliva, a stranger's?

Saliva, Kevin McHale's?

Semen, your own?

Semen, Kevin McHale's?

Vomit?

Bile?

Liquid feces, 50% your own, 50% Kevin McHale's?

WHAT'S YOUR PRICE!?

The Name Game

Would you... change your first name to "Doodatron" for $500,000? What about your last name?

Which of the following names would you change your name to and go by for $500,000?

Scrotal McGee?

Johnny Ballcluster?

Milkbags Maximus?

Extrava Gantlabia?

The "Formerly Known as Prince" symbol?

The sound of a handful of change hitting the table?

What is the weirdest name you'd change yours to for $500,000?

WHAT'S YOUR PRICE!?

In Good Company

Would you... kiss the person to your left on the lips for $20? To the right? Either on the top of the breast for $40? On the side of the neck for $60? On the taint for $500?

Would you... take a punch in the gut from the person on your left for $100? On your right? From the first stranger you see?

Would you... kiss the next stranger you see on the lips for $100? Decide before you see him/her.

Would you... arm wrestle everyone here, winner takes $50?

WHAT'S YOUR PRICE!?

Pet Project

How much would you pay... for a pet panda cub?
A pet Gizmo from *Gremlins*? A pet Transformer?

Would you... eat your own cat or dog for $500,000?
Five million dollars? Fifty million dollars? What's your price?

Would you... die to keep your pet alive?

Would you... have sex with your dog or cat to keep it from being put
to sleep? Your hamster? A three-way with your tortoise and three-toed sloth?

WHAT'S YOUR PRICE!?

Prediction? Pain

Would you... let Barry Bonds take a full baseball bat swing into your gut for $10,000? $100,000? How much for a shot into your head?

Would you... jump out a second-story window for $1,000? $5,000?

Would you... jump out of a third-story window for $50,000? $100,000?

Would you... hammer a nail through the back of your hand for $10,000? $50,000?

Would you... spend one night in a coffin filled with fire ants for $10,000? $100,000? $400,000?

WHAT'S YOUR PRICE!?

Mixed Blessings

Would you... want the writing prowess of Shakespeare if you could only write commercials and print ads for Reebok?

Would you... want the painting prowess of Van Gogh if you had to be a court sketch artist? A bar mitzvah caricaturist? Would you want his abilities if you had to have his psyche as well?

Would you... want the sculpting ability of Michelangelo if you had to work in the medium of feces?

Would you... want the talent of LeBron James if you could only play against 7-year-old kids?

Would you... give your 4-year-old daughter DD breast implants for $1,000,000?

Yes, I would—David Gomberg

I know it's not necessarily the most noble parental choice, but imagine the life you could provide for your child. Private schools. International travel. A personal minstrel. And the truth is a 4-year-old with implants will just look chubby. Probably until she hits 15 years of age at which point the breasts are an asset for improving social standing. So she can't play tennis. Big deal. She won't need it since the compounded interest in her savings account will buy her way into Harvard, where she'll easily be the hottest one there. God forgive me.

No thanks—Justin Heimberg

It's a health thing if nothing else. Your 4-year-old will have chronic bloody noses from the constant toppling due to her disproportionate weight distribution. You better fill those jugs with hydrogen or she'll spend half her childhood on the ground. The poor thing will never even learn to tie her shoes for lack of a clear eyeline. After experiencing her three-headed childhood, the prematurely developed adolescent is destined to become the class slut and will have no need to develop her mind. So buy her a spot at Harvard, and there she will be, the school's slutty airhead, compensating for bad grades with promiscuity, bouncing about the quad in her extra-support bra and untied shoes.

WHAT'S YOUR PRICE!?

Chapter Six

Cool and Unusual Punishment

The Deity is angry. And you wouldn't like him when he's angry. Because he's a real dick. Just a major A-hole. And an A-hole with power is the worst kind of A-hole. Unfortunately, today, the Deity's deep and wrathful gaze has ensnared you in its tractor beam. He has plans for you to work out his issues. It's going to be a long painful day.

Would you rather...

remove your two front teeth with a bottle opener

OR

pierce your ears, nose, and navel with a hole-puncher?

Would you rather...

be pressed to death in a giant waffle grill

OR

be blended to death?

Would you rather...

experience a brain freeze (literally) *OR* heart break (literally)?

have porcelain skin (literally) *OR* hair of gold (literally)?

be tickled to death (literally) *OR* have a spiked mining hammer slammed down into the top of your skull (literally)?

Would you rather...

eat a cotton candy entirely made from belly lint

OR

suck on a human eyeball Jawbreaker for one minute?

YOU MUST CHOOSE!

83

Would you rather spend an 18-hour car ride with...

Richard Simmons *OR* Spencer from *The Hills*?

fitness celebrity John Basedow *OR* Omarosa from *The Apprentice*?

Bruce Banner *OR* a flatulent cocker spaniel?

Dr. Phil *OR* Courtney Love ?

Would you rather fight to the death...

1 Fozzie Bear *OR* 100 GI Joe action figures?

50 Fry Guys *OR* 50 remote control cars?

the Cocoa Puffs Bird *OR* the Noid?

500 fabric softener sheets *OR* 500 dreidels?

100 cups of coffee *OR* 30 watermelons?

Would you rather...

pass a kidney stone the size and shape of a GoBot

OR

a Koosh ball?

Would you rather...

have all your toenails slowly peeled off

OR

have your tonsils Dustbustered out?

YOU MUST CHOOSE!

Would you rather...

BE BEATEN TO DEATH WITH TINKER TOYS

OR

KILLED IN AN AVALANCHE OF D&D DICE?

Would you rather...

have a bowl of tapeworm "linguini"

OR

a slice of pizza topped with recently pulled teeth "pine nuts" and dried scab "pepperoni"?

Would you rather...

enter a cave and be attacked by thousands of Wacky WallWalkers

OR

be assaulted and killed by living toy Army Men?

Would you rather...

have a scoop of vanilla ice cream topped with pubic hair trimmings

OR

a steaming slice of apple pie warmed with the flatulence of 1,000 chili-eating beer-drinkers?

YOU MUST CHOOSE!

88

Would you rather be stuck on a crowded bus with...

Real World reality "stars" **OR** decaying corpses?

The Brat Pack **OR** the characters from *Fraggle Rock*?

braggadocious upholsterers **OR** jaded warlocks?

bawdy accordion players **OR** alluring zoologists?

wistful Foot Locker employees **OR** pussy-whipped Green Berets?

Would you rather...

have all of your hook-ups displayed prominently in YouTube videos

OR

all your masturbatory fantasies printed as a Sunday Comic in explicit detail?

Would you rather...

be churned to death by a hard-hearted Amish giant

OR

be bombarded by a never-ending barrage of ping pong overhead slams?

YOU MUST CHOOSE!

Would you rather...

slide naked down a fireman's pole covered with tacks into a pool of scotch

OR

cheese-grate the skin off your left forearm?

Would you rather...

all of your drunken phone calls be recorded and played back on a popular radio station

OR

have all your love letters and emails posted on Google's homepage?

Would you rather be stuck on a stalled bus with...

coked up Hollywood types *OR* obese Hare Krishnas?

incontinent Labradors *OR* the paparazzi?

forlorn albinos *OR* nosy pirates?

manic-depressive nuns *OR* autistic rodeo clowns?

condescending cobblers *OR* sullen blacksmiths?

articulate half-orcs *OR* dizzy Erin Gray clones?

YOU MUST CHOOSE!

91

Would you rather...

BE EXTRUDED THROUGH A SPAGHETTI MACHINE

OR

BE BURIED ALIVE IN A PIT OF PLAY-DOH?

Would you rather...

dive head first off a 15 meter high-diving board into an empty pool

OR

drink a tall glass of liquid nitrogen?

Would you rather...

have you parents walk in on you while you are having sex

OR

walk in on them?

Would you rather...

chew a used condom as gum for an hour

OR

suck on a pig fetus for ten minutes?

Would you rather...

roll down a hill in a barrel full of thumb tacks

OR

have a live scorpion inserted into your intestines?

Would you rather...

have Roger Federer forehand your face at full force

OR

have Tiger Woods take a tee-shot to your teeth?

YOU MUST CHOOSE!

Would you rather...

EAT EVERY OBJECT IN THE DICTIONARY BETWEEN "GHOST" AND "GRAY"

OR

BETWEEN "BLIMP" AND "BROWN"?

Would you rather...

blend your foot and imbibe the result

OR

castrate yourself with a toe nail clipper?

Would you rather...

be pumped with water until you burst

OR

be dehydrated to death by a giant one of those infomercial beef-jerky-making machines?

Would you... drink poison ivy tea for $15,000?

Would you... use six squirts of poison ivy Afrin nasal spray for $12,000?

Would you... use two-ply poison ivy toilet paper for $27,000?

Would you... put in poison ivy-lined contact lenses for an hour for $30,000?

Would you... rinse with poison ivy mouthwash for $6,000?

Would you... wear a poison ivy yarmulke for $100?

YOU MUST CHOOSE!

The Deity has imprisoned you in a closed room. You are in a fight to the death. All enemies are hostile.

Would you rather fight...

3 possessed lawnmowers *OR* the cast of *Dawson's Creek*?

one vicious werewolf *OR* 6 bashful vampires?

extremely sleepy ninjas *OR* post-diet sumo wrestlers?

a real life incarnation of every team nickname of the NFC *OR* AFC?

Would you rather...

have your lips drawn and quartered

OR

have each of your fingers bent back until they snapped?

(For *Star Trek* nerds only)
Would you rather...

room with the evil Captain Kirk from Episode 27

OR

have sex with a Mugatu beast from Episode 45?

YOU MUST CHOOSE!

Would you rather...

have Wesley Snipes catch you picking your nose

OR

fall down in front of Edward James Olmos?

Would you rather...

as a guy, be licking a woman's breast only to discover a 3-inch hair on her nipple

OR

be kissing her lower back only to discover a tattoo of Roger Ebert?

Would you rather...

administer Tabasco sauce eye drops

OR

rub a steak knife against your gums?

Would you rather...

take a power drill in the Adam's apple

OR

fill your pants with raw meat and kick a pit bull in the side?

YOU MUST CHOOSE!

Cool and Unusual Punishment

Would you rather...

have your fingernails peeled off, one by one

OR

put your mouth around a high powered sprinkler for 15 minutes?

Would you rather...

remove your heart with a staple remover

OR

be unable to circumvent the "lather, rinse repeat" instructions on the back of shampoo bottles, perpetually shampooing yourself until starvation?

Would you rather...

make out with someone in a dark club only to find when the lights go on that their mouth is covered in open puss-filled cold sores

OR

that it's your mother-in-law? Father-in-law? Bill Wennington?

Would you rather...

have your nipples gnawed off by a swarm of termites

OR

sit on an umbrella and then open it?

YOU MUST CHOOSE!

Would you rather fight to the death...

50 remote control planes *OR* 1,000 hamsters?

1,000 sloths *OR* 80 penguins?

possessed office supplies *OR* possessed deli meats?

Koala bears *OR* Berenstain Bears?

25,000,000 starving tapeworms *OR* the starting line-up for the New York Liberty?

Would you rather...

receive a red-hot cattle prod throat culture

OR

a sulfuric acid enema?

Would you rather...

be tossed headfirst out the window 40 floors up

OR

be placed in a pit that was slowly filled with wet cement? Sand? Marbles? Lee Majors action figures?

Would you rather...

spontaneously combust

OR

spontaneously turn into Harriet Beecher Stowe?

YOU MUST CHOOSE!

Would you rather...

have your mom bring a blacklight into your room to reveal the various sexual fluids strewn about

OR

have to call tech support because you were surfing porn and more and more porn sites and pop-ups keep coming up on screen and so you have to talk through the problem with specifics and you're like "this website Assparade.com comes up and when I try to close it, an ad for Peter North's Volume pills comes up," and your mom comes in, and you try to close all the sites and ads real quick, like you're playing missile command on Atari, but every time you close a window, another porn ad pops open, and it's like trying to cut off the Hydra's heads, and you turn off the monitor but it's too late, and you realize that maybe it's time to move out of your parents' house?

Would you rather...

have just eaten rice only to find out they were maggots

OR

be sucking on a endless succulent strand of spaghetti only to find out it's the umbilical cord of a woman who's just given birth?

Would you rather...

be caught masturbating by your grandmother

OR

vice-versa?

YOU MUST CHOOSE!

Would you rather...

CHAIN-SMOKE 100 CIGARETTES NASALLY

OR

TONGUE CLEAN 10 BLOCKS WORTH OF NEW YORK CITY PUBLIC PHONE MOUTHPIECES?

Would you rather...

stick your tongue in an electric pencil sharpener

OR

have an ant crawl up your urethra Franklin and lay hundreds of eggs?

Would you rather...

perform oral sex on a chronic flatulator

OR

give Forest Whitaker a handjob?

Would you rather...

find a used condom at the bottom of your vanilla latte

OR

find a dirty panty liner under the cheese in your tuna melt?

Would you rather...

forcibly floss your teeth with rusty barbed wire

OR

bob for apples in a Long John Silver deep fryer?

YOU MUST CHOOSE!

Would you rather...

saw through your thumbs with a hack saw

OR

slice off your nipples with a deli meat-slicer?

(Borg only)
Would you rather...

be assimilated

OR

be assimilated?

Things to consider: Resistance is futile

Would you rather...

shave your left eyeball with a Gillette Sensor

OR

pour a gallon of boiling water down your mouth?

Would you rather...

be pureed in a giant blender

OR

be tanned to death in an over-charged tanning bed?

YOU MUST CHOOSE!

Would you rather...

FIGHT TO THE DEATH...
15 GEESE

OR

100 PILLSBURY DOUGHBOYS?

Would you rather...

fight to the death 15 geese *OR* 100 Pillsbury Doughboys?

Bring It, Boys—David Gomberg

It'd be great fighting the Doughboys. You'd feel like an all-powerful giant, flinging the bread-men off your body like flies, kneading them to misshapen embarrassment. Tearing their doughy flesh apart and devouring it like a monster. Some may say the Doughboy cannot be killed, that it re-collects itself like a blob or that metallically gelatinous guy in *Terminator 2*. But there are fool-proof ways of killing Doughboys: the toaster. One by one to the chamber of death they will go, the assault of their doughy fists feeling like a gentle massage.

Geese, Please—Justin Heimberg

Gomberg, you ignorant slut. We know the biology of geese. They are a known quantity. What twisted anatomy dwells within the dark magic of the Doughboy we cannot say. And you forget about the most deadly weapon of the Doughboy, suffocation. They will stuff one another into your mouth, wrap tight around your nostrils, fusing, Voltron-like, into one massive doughboy. Remember there are 100 of them. You may volley and kick a dozen or so away at a time, but they will engulf you and you will lose your life in a doughy coffin. Fifteen geese is manageable. They can peck and snap and flap annoyingly. But their necks are tantalizingly breakable. Yes, I will break their necks, one by one, and soon the world will be mine....
(Maniacal cackle.)

YOU MUST CHOOSE!

Chapter Seven

Not-Quite-Super Powers

Lucky you. The Deity is in good spirits. Turns out, he was right all along. It is spelled "deity," not "diety." He's bubbling over with happiness and wants to share it with you by bestowing upon you one of two peculiar, if not super, powers. What you do with your newfound power is up to you. As always, you must choose...

Would you rather...

be able to fart out Polaroid photos

OR

have self-tying sneakers?

Would you rather...

be able to fight masterfully with origami creations *OR* your keys?

your own spit *OR* your own hair?

tortillas *OR* your computer mouse?

Would you rather...

be able to give someone else the extra weight you would typically put on after you eat poorly

OR

be able to give your hangovers to someone else after you drink?

Would you rather have...

have the ability to empty your bladder by "beaming" your urine to a toilet like in *Star Trek*

OR

be capable of shooting pubic "quills" in self-defense like a porcupine?

YOU MUST CHOOSE!

Would you rather...

BE A TRANSFORMER WHO CAN CHANGE INTO A GEORGE FOREMAN GRILL

OR

A YARMULKE?

Would you rather...

HAVE A KETCHUP DISPENSING NAVEL

OR

A PENCIL SHARPENING NOSTRIL?

Would you rather...

be able to cool coffee to a drinkable level with merely one blow

OR

be able to miraculously neatly consume sloppy joes?
Things to consider: career options

Would you rather...

be able to highlight with your finger

OR

be able to induce nosebleeds in people on live TV?
Things to consider: political debates, news anchors, NBA games

Would you rather...

be able to do a perfect rendition of Nena's "99 Red Balloons" by cracking your knuckles

OR

be able to perform a masterfully timed routine of Abbott and Costello's "Who's on First?" in sign language?

Would you rather...

be able to fly one inch of the ground

OR

turn your left foot invisible?

YOU MUST CHOOSE!

Would you rather...

be able to inflate your muscles to look strong but have no actual exceptional strength

OR

be extremely strong, but have the body of this guy...

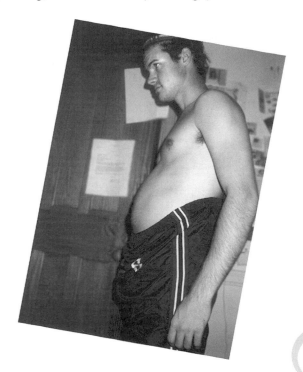

YOU MUST CHOOSE!

Would you rather...

your farts be literally silent but deadly

OR

audible and capable of inducing 2nd degree burns?

Would you rather...

be able to legally notarize documents by biting down on them

OR

be incredibly charming from 3:32 pm to 3:35pm every day?

Would you rather...

be a Transformer who can transform into a toaster *OR* hairdryer?

a Trapper Keeper notebook *OR* that foot measuring device?

a cement parking space block *OR* Geraldine Ferraro?

Would you rather...

be able to blow tranquilizer dart snot-rockets

OR

have a detachable Fu Manchu mustache/boomerang?

YOU MUST CHOOSE!

Would you rather...

be Dr. Grass, a superhero whose power is to induce grass stains

OR

The Summarizer, a superhero who can clearly and concisely express any given situation?

Would you rather...

be able to record your sex dreams while you sleep for viewing while you're awake

OR

be able to save all of your memories for safe-keeping and easy recall on a USB flash drive?

Would you rather...

speak in surround sound

OR

have the ability to transform your sexual partner's face into that of the celebrity of your choice for one minute per day?

Would you rather...

have the power of telekinesis but only to alter pants

OR

be able to read minds, but only with people named Deandre?

YOU MUST CHOOSE!

Would you rather...

have nunchucks for hands

OR

ice-making nostrils?

Would you rather...

have an inkblot tattoo that changes every day

OR

be able to "Voltron" with your friends into a giant?

Would you rather...

have a Google in your brain

OR

be able to delete things on Wikipedia and make them really disappear?

(Comic book nerds only)
Would you rather...

have Nightcrawler's ability to "Bamf"

OR

Batman's ability to generate visual onomatopoeia upon punches, kicks, and collisions?
Things to consider: PWOOF!, WHAPPP!, DORPPP!

YOU MUST CHOOSE!

Would you rather...

HAVE A TAPE DISPENSING MOUTH

OR

A BOTTLE OPENING NOSTRIL?

Would you rather...

produce helium-filled feces *OR* TNT-filled feces?

capsule-shelled feces *OR* perfectly cubed feces?

feces that fades away in two minutes *OR* fortune feces (feces that have a secret fortune written in the middle of each piece)?

Would you rather...

have eyes that can tint themselves like light-sensitive sunglasses

OR

hands that can exude lubricant upon command?

Would you rather...

have raspberry scented B.O.

OR

have Tic Tac boogers?

Would you rather...

have the power to project a Jell-O force field

OR

be able to perfectly gauge cream and sugar amounts by eyeing the color of your coffee?

YOU MUST CHOOSE!

Would you rather...

HAVE YOUR DREAMS
WRITTEN AND DIRECTED BY
THE MAKERS OF THE MATRIX

OR

BY THE MAKERS OF
GIRLS GONE WILD?

Would you rather...

be able to simulate the voice of anybody you meet

OR

simulate the hair?

Would you rather...

be able to achieve orgasm at will

OR

be able to make anyone other than you achieve orgasm at your will?

Things to consider: public speakers, staff meetings, sporting events

Would you rather...

be able to consume fatty foods without gaining weight

OR

be able to have unprotected sex without getting sexual diseases?

Things to consider: Syphilis, Chlamydia, hot fudge, gravy fries, cheese balls

Would you rather...

have Bette Davis eyes

OR

Charles Manson eyes?

YOU MUST CHOOSE!

Would you rather...

be able to communicate with animals, but only the nerds

OR

be able to read people's minds but only when they are thinking about aluminum siding topics and issues?

Would you rather...

have taste buds all over your body

OR

have a malleable stress-ball head?

Would you rather...

have an anus that can function as a DustBuster

OR

nipples that can act as universal light dimmers?

Would you rather...

have a tongue that doubles as a retractable tape measure

OR

have a GPS built into your crotch?

YOU MUST CHOOSE!

Would you rather...

BE ABLE TO FIGHT AND KILL MASTERFULLY WITH YO-YOS

OR

WITH FRISBEES?

Would you rather...

have an ever-changing tattoo that takes the form of whatever image you will it to be

OR

be able to psychically see anybody's Internet browser history when looking at them?

Would you rather...

have puma-like reactions with the remote control when watching something dirty, and someone walks into the room, and you need to change it

OR

have expert precision with the cheek-kiss greeting?

Would you rather...

have a stable of remarkably sympathetic woodland creatures to confide in about romantic desires and dreams

OR

be capable of ending any relationship tension-free with no ensuing debate or discussion by pulling out a red card like in soccer?
Things to consider: yellow card warnings

YOU MUST CHOOSE!

Would you rather...

have the ability to talk clearly while dentists are working on your teeth

OR

permission to talk dirty?

The Deity has decided he might want to take over the world (depending on his schedule). To aid him on his quest, he's decided to make you a supervillain.

Would you rather be...

The Laminator

OR

Dr. Humidity?

Would you rather be...

Rash Man (annoys foes with minor skin irritations)

OR

The Tenderizer (softens foes with rapid strikes of a mallet)?

Would you rather...

have Gatorade saliva

OR

argyle irises?

YOU MUST CHOOSE!

Would you rather...

have the power to switch your emotions on and off

OR

be able to fully comprehend written material just by sniffing the words?

Things to consider: reading in the library/on subway, leadership potential

Would you rather...

be able to fast-forward life

OR

rewind it?

Things to consider: pelbin

Would you rather...

be able to increase the intensity/frequency of nearby throbbing objects

OR

be able to flatulate to the tune of "When the Saints Go Marching In"?

Would you rather...

have elastic lips

OR

adjustable palm lines?

Things to consider: messing with psychics

YOU MUST CHOOSE!

Would you rather...

be able to insist on paying for the check but never actually get stuck with it

OR

know exactly what the person on the other end of the phone looks like simply by hearing their voice?

Would you rather...

be able to will your pot-belly to other parts of your body

OR

be able to murmur in twelve languages?

Things to consider: this question excerpted from Plato's *Republic*

(Orthodox Jews only)

Would you rather..

have nice full flowing payois

OR

always know where the matzo is hidden?

Would your rather...

never miss throwing a quarter into a tollbooth basket

OR

be able to defecate miniature models of famous Rodin sculptures?

130

YOU MUST CHOOSE!

Would you rather...

have an ass-fax

OR

a Phillips head screwdriver outie belly button?

Pro Ass-Fax (anti-screwdriver-navel)—David Gomberg

How many times did you wish you had a port-a-fax? You're at home and you need to send some forms to your accountant. No more trips to Kinko's. Just drop your pants, insert, and enjoy. You could be a spy, a war correspondent, anything. You dream it, you can ass-fax it. On the other hand, the screwdriver outie belly button is a curse, not a power. The stiff rod of the driver stem is firmly fixed to your abdomen. This means to turn a screw you will have to turn your entire body. That is an almost impossible motion. Approaching screws from on top and the side is awkward and painful, so your power is little more than freakishly ornamental. Do yourself a favor and sit on some paper and dial.

Pro-screwdriver navel (Anti-ass-fax)—Justin Heimberg

With the ass-fax, my problem isn't so much sending as receiving. You're sitting around in a Starbucks, enjoying a latte, and then all of the sudden a sheet of paper begins to emerge from your crack. If you're seated, you'll need to get up to allow for the emergence of the sheet (or sheets). And if you're wearing pants, there will be an inevitable paper jam in your anal cavity. Unless you're into that sort of thing, that is bad news. By the time you adjourn to the bathroom, your fax will be crumpled, torn and covered with fecal matter. As will your sphincter. Paper cuts are bad enough on your hand. Leave the ass-faxing to professionals.

YOU MUST CHOOSE!

Not-Quite-Super Powers

131

Chapter Eight

Random Play

The Deity is on random play. He is octopolar in mood, and there is no telling what might come out of his mouth... or the rest of him for that matter.

Would you rather...

always have to drive half the speed limit

OR

twice the speed limit?

Would you rather...

never be able to open your mouth when throwing up

OR

have your nostrils and lips seal shut when you sneeze?

Would you rather...

have a stutter at the end of every word-d-d-d

OR

have written fuck! Tourrette's Syndrome balls!?

Things to ass-munch! consider: power point dildo! presentations, love letters cunttrap!; shit-ass!; fuck!; dickdangle!

Would you rather...

have hair that is 4 feet long

OR

hair of normal length but with each hair having a one-inch diameter?

Things to consider: increased head weight, specially designed combs

YOU MUST CHOOSE!

Would you rather...

take 900 consecutive punches to the taint by Chuck Norris

OR

have your eyelids pulled taut and cut off by nail-clippers?

Things to consider: likelihood of survival after taint pummeling, sleeping, bloody tears (for both options), literally having the shit beat out of you

Would you rather...

have a self-refilling coffee mug that keeps your sugar/cream ratio perfect

OR

have throwing star business cards?

Would you rather...

be able to drink only from water fountains

OR

subsist solely on any free samples you can score at supermarkets?

Would you rather...

be bcc'ed on every e-mail to and from your significant other *OR* your mom?

Paris Hilton *OR* Perez Hilton?

Gary Gnu *OR* Steve Winwood?

YOU MUST CHOOSE!

Would you rather...

have hair that can harden into a helmet at your command

OR

pubic hair that can harden into a cup?

Would you rather...

have permanent Milwaukee's Best aftertaste

OR

have an odd palsy where you always walk as if you're laying down a bunt?

Would you rather...

be able to induce instant five o'clock shadow

OR

be able to sense farts 30 seconds before they happen (like a Spideysense)?

Would you rather...

find out all of your moments in front of a mirror in the past week have been secretly filmed and broadcasted on YouTube

OR

that the previous 30 minutes of discussion has been secretly filmed and broadcasted on YouTube?

YOU MUST CHOOSE!

Would you rather...

HAVE WORMS FOR EYELASHES

OR

CORDUROY SKIN?

Left, Right, or Center

Would you rather...

for five dollars, engage in a staring contest with the person on your left (clockwise)

OR

engage in a best 3 out of 5 of Rock, Paper, Scissors to the person to your right (counterclockwise)?

Things to consider: Make it happen.

Would you rather...

dry-hump the person next to you (clockwise)

OR

be manually stimulated by the person to your right (counterclockwise)?

Things to consider: Make it happen?

YOU MUST CHOOSE!

Would you rather...

have Wii controls that work for real people in front of you (voodoo style)

OR

have everything you write in Wikipedia become true?

Ten minutes before your death, would you rather find out...

there is no God

OR

that this whole time the term "au jus" translated to "ass juice"?

Would you rather...

only be able to hear words spoken by females

OR

males?

Would you rather...

fight to the death 12 angry rabbis

OR

34 Mr. Peanuts?

YOU MUST CHOOSE!

Would you rather...

LIE DOWN NAKED ON A BENIHANA TABLE

OR

HAVE YOUR MOUTH STRETCHED AROUND THE PART OF A LAWNMOWER WHERE THE GRASS SPITS OUT WHILE IT MOWS HIGH GRASS?

Random Play

Would you rather...

your neck be as long as your torso

OR

your torso be as short as your neck?

Things to consider: driving (accelerating quickly, phone books for seat, need for sun roof)

Would you... have sex with Jessica Biel if there was 1 in 10 chance that her vagina would suddenly turn to a blender?

Would you... put your penis in a glory hole for $60,000 if you were told there was an equal chance of your mother, Jenna Jameson, and Greg Gumbel being on the other side? (You would never find out, nor would they.)

Would you rather...

have a bad acid trip in Amish Country **OR** in Bed Bath and Beyond?

in Home Depot **OR** Sharper Image?

while watching *Teletubbies* **OR** *Deal or No Deal*?

YOU MUST CHOOSE!

Would you rather...

be able to delete memories in your mind as if files on a computer

OR

be able to network to other people's brains like on a computer so you could share knowledge (provided they agreed to give you access)?

Would you rather...

sneeze inward

OR

fart inward?

Would you rather...

have that photo-flash-induced red-eye appearance in real life

OR

at all holiday parties, become incorrigibly convinced you are working at a 1920s meat-packing factory?

Would you rather...

have a two inch underbite

OR

a two inch overbite? Sidebite?

YOU MUST CHOOSE!

Would you rather...

have finite amounts of emotions (e.g. resentment, sadness, happiness) like various color printer ink cartridges

OR

as you drink, become incredibly adamant about the superiority of isosceles triangles to the point of starting fights?

Things to consider: Scalene?! Are you fuckin' kidding me?!

Would you rather...

sleep in 4 minute intervals (4 minutes awake, 4 minutes asleep, and so on)

OR

have multiple personality disorder consisting of personas: surly dockworker, pompous cobbler, and retarded ringmaster?

Would you rather...

only be able to open your eyes 1/8 of an inch

OR

only be able to open your mouth 1/8 of an inch?

Would you rather...

be raised by dogs *OR* chimps?

angels *OR* the Harlem Globetrotters?

9 year olds *OR* the New Kids on the Block?

144

YOU MUST CHOOSE!

Would you rather...

have five 2-inch penises located in your general crotch area

OR

three 4-inch penises, with one located on your knee, one on the small of your back, and one branching from the aforementioned penis that is on your knee?
Things to consider: dual input ability, orgies, attempts at multiple orgasm

Would you rather...

have permanently undulating belly fat

OR

have an uncontrollable romantic attraction to heads of lettuce?
Things to consider: shopping, employment as a dinner theater entertainer

Would you rather...

have a type of anorexia where the left side of your body appears incredibly fat to you

OR

have a severe phobia of 47 degree angles?
Things to consider: How would you dress?; brief moments of panic during see-saw play; geometry class

Would you rather live in a world...

comprised of Lego

OR

Play-Doh?

YOU MUST CHOOSE!

Would you rather...

have a nice timbre to your voice but always be trying to figure out which way the wind is blowing

OR

cultivate a sense of gravitas but compulsively hit yourself in the balls with great force every ten minutes?

Would you rather...

be able to italicize printed lettering by sheer force of will and a concentrated stare

OR

be able to skip at just below Olympic sprinting pace?

Would you rather...

have your tonsils removed with a fork and steak knife

OR

place your ankles on a train track and let them be run over by Amtrak's Acela Express?

Would you rather...

have the *SportsCenter* guys do a full report (complete with highlights) on ESPN whenever you return from a date

OR

whenever you have a bowel movement?

YOU MUST CHOOSE!

Would you rather...

have to always drive on highways "playing Pac-Man" – where your car straddles the dotted white lines that divide lanes

OR

have to drive with your seat reclined at a 150 degree angle?

Would you rather...

have strobe light headlights

OR

have to arm wrestle an increasingly strong gearshift to get into next gear?

Would you rather...

have a horn that could, on command, project a hologram of a big middle finger

OR

have you car alarm beep sound be the *Law & Order* sound?

Things to consider: inadvertent summoning of Sam Waterson

Would you rather...

have a radio that was stuck in time to June 19th, 1983

OR

on a current morning zoo show?

YOU MUST CHOOSE!

Would you rather...

have to plug yourself in every few hours to recharge before you shut down as you would a laptop

OR

only be able to travel by means of rickshaw?

Things to consider: camping trips, car adapters

Would you rather...

permanently share your bedroom with 200 mosquitoes *OR* 5 boa constrictors?

25 black widow spiders *OR* 3 landmines (you know where they are)?

the ghost of George Washington Carver *OR* heavy metal band Pantera?

Would you rather...

have a pimento permanently housed in each nostril

OR

have hairy gums?

Would you rather...

have everything you say have an interrogative inflection?

OR

your have the random sentence words in out come order?

YOU MUST CHOOSE!

Would you rather...

DRIP HOT WAX ONTO YOUR EYES

OR

TWIST A CORKSCREW INTO YOUR BELLY BUTTON?

Would you rather...

have to use every page in this book as toilet paper

OR

have to smoke every page in this book?

Would you rather...

have Internet chat sex (including video of faces but with no volume) with someone who is hot as hell but is just an egregiously awful speller

OR

someone who is decent looking and has great writing panache and grammar skills?

Things to consider: I wunt to nale you. I am masterbating to a clymacks. Are you into annul?

Would you rather...

have a delusional paranoia where you reflexively try to perform CPR whenever you see anyone sleeping

OR

have farts that release explosive red dye similar to the dye packs found in bags of money during bank robberies?

Things to consider: worried launderers, resuscitation attempts being mistaken for sexual advances

YOU MUST CHOOSE!

Would you rather have a tattoo of...

an illusion of knee high tube socks **OR** an illusion of a yarmulke?

a "tramp stamp" **OR** "taint paint"?

a large back tattoo of the Atari 2600 game *Breakout* **OR** of a croissant?

Would you rather...

be cursed where all your dry cleaned shirts are returned to you as Don Drysdale #53 replica jerseys

OR

have a speech disorder where you invariably start every sentence with the phrase "Rumor has it..."?

If forced by threat of death, would you rather...

cough "Boring!" during a wedding ceremony of a close relative

OR

wear an oversized hockey jersey and one of those foam "Number 1" hands to the funeral of a family friend?

YOU MUST CHOOSE!

If forced by threat of death, during a business meeting, would you rather...

have to use the phrase "cumload" four times

OR

have to wear those blue and red 3D glasses for the entire meeting?

Things to consider: Subtly injecting the profanity in corporate context: "We had a cumload of response from our new marketing campaign." "Let's be proactive and get a cumload of buzz going." "Marsha, is that a cumload on your shirt?"

Would you rather...

have a sexual partner that talks to you like a motivational speaker during sex

OR

that talks to you like a "bad cop" interrogator?

Would you rather...

have sex with Victoria Beckham if she gained 60 pounds

OR

if she lost 20 pounds?

YOU MUST CHOOSE!

Would you rather...

have sex with Johnny Depp if he put on 75 pounds for a movie role

OR

Sean Penn if he became a heroin addict for a movie role?

Would you rather...

have sex with someone who has the butt of Kim Kardashian and the face of Kim Jong Il

OR

the body of Halle Berry and the head of Frankenberry?

Would you rather have sex with...

crazy, chunky Britney circa 2008 *OR* sane, nubile Britney circa 2003?

Reese Witherspoon *OR* Jennifer Garner?

Paula Abdul *OR* Megan Fox if she were missing an arm? A leg? An eye? Missing all of the above?

Carrie Underwood *OR* *Top Chef's* Padma Lakshmi?

Things to consider: Salman Rushdie tapped that.

YOU MUST CHOOSE!

Would you rather have sex with...

Donald Trump *OR* Vince McMahon?

Topher Grace *OR* LeBron James?

Seth Rogen *OR* Mario Lopez?

Dennis Kucinich if he had a 10-inch penis *OR* John Edwards if he had a 3-inch penis?

Would you rather...

get to 2nd base with Jessica Simpson

OR

go all the way with Tara Reid?

Would you rather...

get to first base with Angelina Jolie

OR

third base with Helen Hunt?

Would you rather...

get hit by a pitch with Monica Bellucci

OR

foul off a couple close ones and then strike out looking with Briana Banks?

YOU MUST CHOOSE!

156

Would you rather...

be able to change one physical attribute of your spouse with that change having the opposite effect on you (i.e., the larger you make her breasts, the more concave yours become)

OR

be able to do the same thing but with a mental trait?
Things to consider: What trait would you choose?

Would you rather...

have access to a MySpace-like online community site where it was revealed who everyone has had sex with and who they have had sex with, and so on

OR

not?

Would you rather have a hallucination of...

your parents melting *OR* your parents having sex?

your own death *OR* John Madden bathing?

being attacked by staplers *OR* being attacked by a swarm of Post-it notes?

YOU MUST CHOOSE!

Would you rather...

gargle vomit mouthwash

OR

inhale Krazy Glue nasal spray?

Would you rather...

have an impulse control problem that causes you to perform ten wild pelvic thrusts every hour on the hour

OR

be unable to refrain from "sacking" the elderly as soon as you see them?

Things to consider: business presentations, going to a retirement home

Would you rather have a hallucination...

that the snack you are eating is turning into eyeballs *OR* your palm lines are turning into worms?

that you are being followed by Charles Grodin *OR* that you are being dry-humped by two Koala Bears?

that your shadow is trying to kill you *OR* that your tongue is?

that your mole is a laser sighting from a gun *OR* that your jewelry is constricting?

of Jon Voight setting up a badminton net *OR* Mike Huckabee relaxing on a bench reading the paper?

YOU MUST CHOOSE!

158

Would you rather...

die by defenestration

OR

by fenestration?

Would you rather...

have legs of Jell-O, literally

OR

have diarrhea of the mouth, literally?

As a super villain, would you rather be...

The Registrar *OR* The Launderer?

The Fifth Year Senior *OR* The Male Cheerleader?

The Unitarian *OR* The Ubiquitous Shirtless Guy You Always See On *Cops*?

The Heckler *OR* The Doorman?

Things to consider: Imagine the uniform, powers, alter egos, and catchphrases for your character

YOU MUST CHOOSE!

Would you lather...

(What began as a Japanese man's mispronunciation became an idea unto itself)

Would you lather... a hippopotamus?

Would you lather... Condoleezza Rice?

Would you lather... the Fry guys?

Would you lather... a chinchilla?

Would you lather... Jason Bateman?

Would you lather... the scalp of Emmanuel Lewis?

YOU MUST CHOOSE!

Would you rather...

AS A SUPER VILLAIN, BE CAPTAIN CONDIMENT

OR

THE MALE CHEERLEADER?

Would you rather...

have all your eye blinks last ten seconds **OR** have all your yawns last two hours?

Anti-yawn—Justin Heimberg

Two-hour yawns will lead to a paradoxical torture. A catch-22 of the worst sort. Follow the logic, here. You yawn when you are tired. You cannot fall asleep when you are yawning. Ergo, you will never get any sleep. Your two-hour yawns will keep you up in that weird suspended animation-like state that is the yawn. You will then become more and more tired each hour, each day increasingly yawning, increasingly prohibiting sleep. Eventually you will go crazy and wander the streets known as the Yawner, a creature of myth that people both yearn and fear to see. Your mouth will open and close of its own accord, making chewing impossible, until your diet will be all smoothie and the bugs that inevitably will fly into your open yawning mouth. Eventually, hungry, infected with mouth sores, and deprived of sleep, you will yawn yourself to death.

Anti-blink—David Gomberg

We blink often. An average of 20 times per minute, according to the second thing that came up when I Googled it. That means there are only a few seconds between blinks. Do the math. This means your eyes will be closed at a 3:1 ratio. Do the math. 10 seconds closed, 3 seconds open. You are half-blind, not in one eye, and not with bad vision, but half the time. Driving is an impossibility. I mean, do the math. Reading would be too arduous to deal with. You'd always be the one screwing up family pictures. Have you done your math homework? People will always think you are deep in thought and meditation only to emerge with uninteresting shallow thoughts. You'd be a constant blinking disappointment. Do the math. Seriously. Please.

162

Chapter Nine

What's Your Price...?
Part 2

Career Change

For $300,000 a year, would you be...

A proctologist specializing in the obese and hairy?

A phone sex operator for the hard of hearing?

One of those haggard crabbing dudes on those dangerous fishing boats?

James Lipton's personal assistant?

James Lipton's personal masseuse? With "happy ending" included?

Mother's Day

The Deity is giving you full immunity. You'd be masked and never suspected.

Would you... body slam your mom for $30,000?

After the body slam, would you drop the elbow for another $10,000?

Then put her in a figure-four leg lock until she tapped out for another $8,000?

To finish her off, hit her with the Hulk Hogan leg drop for another $3,500?

Offer to help her up and then pull your hand away at the last second and give her the "psych" gesture for $12,000?

All together it comes to $63,500? How far would you go?

$ WHAT'S YOUR PRICE!?

Jewelry

For $5,000 a day, would you...

wear a 5 lb. earring for a week? A 5 lb. nose piercing? A 5 lb. nipple piercing? A 5 lb. Prince Albert? How many days could you go for each?

Would you... wear a tongue piercing that was the size and shape of a golf ball for one week for $32,000?

Would you... wear an earring that was connected to an earring on your mother with a four-foot chain for one week for $80,000? If, for every foot you shorten the chain, the money is doubled: how short would you go?

Would you... wear a barbed wire watchband for a month for $17,000?

Final Implant

Would you... as a man, get DD breast implants for $100,000? C-cups? B-cups?

What if they can be removed after a year? After a month?

What about just one breast implant? On the top of your foot? On the bottom of your foot?

Would you... get breast implants if your significant other promised to get them too, two sizes bigger than your own?

WHAT'S YOUR PRICE!?

Anatomically Incorrect

Would you... for $1,000,000, have a finger removed? Two fingers? Two fingers and a toe? An arm? An ear? Would you have an ear added on for a million?

Would you... if the Deity made it possible, have a third testicle for $100,000? If you received another $50,000 for every additional testicle you accepted, how high would you go?

Things to consider: your nest egg(s); (Women: use "nipple" instead of "testicle.")

Would you... give up one year of your life to have a penis that was 3 inches longer (men) or breasts that were three sizes larger (women)? How many years for how many inches/sizes?

WHAT'S YOUR PRICE!?

WOULD YOU RATHER...? Overstuffed

Would you have sex with Angelina Jolie if she put on 50 lbs.?

100lbs.?

200 lbs.?

300 lbs.?

How high would you go?

Would you have sex with George Clooney if he put on 50 lbs.?

100lbs.?

200lbs.?

300lbs.?

Lost 100 lbs.?

Got a sex change?

WHAT'S YOUR PRICE!?

Punch Bowl

How much would you pay to punch (a clean shot with no repercussions)...

Paula Abdul?

Paris Hilton?

Donald Trump?

Nancy Grace?

George Bush?

Anyone who's ever appeared on the *Real World*?

Celebrity Sex
Leading Men

How much would pay for one steamy night with...

Tom Brady?

Justin Timberlake?

Derek Jeter?

Prince?

Vince Vaughn?

A being that is the top half of Patrick Dempsey and the bottom half of Patrick Ewing?

A trio of fast and furious Pillsbury Doughboys?

Tom Cruise?

Tom Cruise including an hour-long diatribe against prescription medicine?

WHAT'S YOUR PRICE!?

Celebrity Sex
Leading Ladies

How much would pay for one steamy night with...

Jessica Biel?

Jessica Alba?

Jessica Rabbit?

All three of the Jessica's above together?

Jessica Hahn?

Uncle Jesse (*Full House*)?

Uncle Jesse (*Dukes of Hazzard*)?

Would you... have sex with either Uncle Jesse to have sex with both Daisy Dukes (Jessica Simpson and Catherine Bach in her prime)?

Strike a Deal!
On the Job

Negotiate with your friends to find a price to actually do these dares or variations thereof. (Pooling money to give is a good way to make it happen.)

Would you... for one week, change your voice mail message to you doing a freestyle rap of how you can't get to the phone for $2,000 ? Another $300 for beat-boxing. *Strike a deal!*

Would you... for $3,000, plaster your cubicle walls with posters of *Saved by the Bell* stars? Sultry pictures of yourself? A collage of Søren Kierkegaard pictures and Mark Gastineau photos? I would.

Would you... for $800, stuff the crotch of your pants obscenely for the duration of the next big office meeting or school presentation? (Same question for women.) *Strike a deal!*

WHAT'S YOUR PRICE!?

Breaking the Law

Would you... kill a known child molester if you could get away with it?

Would you... kill a mime if you could get away with it? How about a mime whose whole gimmick is miming child molestation?

Would you... commit an armed robbery if you knew you'd never be caught? At a bank? A 7-11? A rich asshole's house?

Would you... steal a CD if you could get away with it? Would you copy eight MP3's from a friend? Does it make a difference how rich the musician is?

WHAT'S YOUR PRICE!?

The Price of Indigestion

Would you... eat a live rat for $1,000? $20,000? $100,000?

Would you... consume a bag full of rusty thumbtacks for $100,000? $1,000,000?
Things to consider: digestion and egress

Would you... blend your left foot in a blender and consume the results for $1,000,000? $10,000,000? $100,000,000?

Would you... eat a Twinkie with a burrowing ant farm inside it for $600? $6,000? What's your price?

WHAT'S YOUR PRICE!?

Worst Birthday Ever

During your child's well-attended fifth birthday party, would you, for $50,000...

Do acid?

    Crack?

        PCP?

            Pot?

                Chain-smoke?

                Get very drunk?

                        Smoke opium and dress up as a demented elderly Asian man?

WHAT'S YOUR PRICE!?

Baby Names!

Don't think, say yes or no!

For $200,000 put in your bank account today, would you name your child...

Romulex?

Doctor?

Litmus?

Keldor?

Assmunch?

Whorey?

95?

Adolph?

Bigballs?

Adolph Bigballs?

Perineum?

The Vindicator of the Damned?

WHAT'S YOUR PRICE!?

Home Sweet Home

Would you... share an apartment with Kevin Federline to lower your rent by $700 a month?

Would you... have bunk beds with Richard Simmons to live free in a $3 million house? Would you take the top or bottom bunk?

Would you... pay a $300 service fee to have your doorbell be changed to Darth Vader's "Imperial March"?

Would you... give up TV if you could have a personal butler?

WHAT'S YOUR PRICE!?

Give It Up!

For $100,000 deposited in your bank account today, which of the following would you give up for life?

Cereal?

Brunch?

Dishwashers?

The left sock?

All of your photos?

Memories of all the TV/movies you have ever seen?

Memories of your cousins?

The word *the*?

Running?

WHAT'S YOUR PRICE!?

The Sporting Life

Would you... pay $5,000 to be able to dunk? $25,000? How high would you go?

Would you... pay $50,000 to be able to run a sub-four-minute mile?

Would you... pay $4,000 for infallible Skee-ball accuracy?

Would you... take Larry Bird's jumpshot but Gary Coleman's physical size?

Would you... pay $1,200 for ruthlessly successful Risk military strategy?

WHAT'S YOUR PRICE!?

The Deity's Tattoo Shop

Each tattoo has a price that represents the money you receive if you get the tattoo (and agree not to have it removed.)

Would you get a tattoo of...

The face of Alex Trebek on your right shoulder... $23,000?

All of your muscles and bones labeled as if you were a diagram in a biology textbook... $290,000?

A Hitler mustache... $700,000

An "I'm with stupid" with an arrow pointing up on your chest... $115,000?

A tattoo of the Deity anywhere... $4,000?
(Send us a photo of your tattoo of the Deity at info@wouldyourather.com and we will post it on wouldyourather.com and possibly publish it in the next book.)

The Chinese symbol for cliché... $8,000?

A full tuxedo... $400,000 (you can get this one removed)? In fact if you do, triple the money.

WHAT'S YOUR PRICE!?

Cavity Search

For $250,000, with no chance of getting caught but with all the physical discomfort, would you anally smuggle from an international airport, for the duration of a flight, and then through U.S. customs...

A prune?

A plum?

A peach?

An orange?

A cantaloupe?

A celery stalk?

35 lbs. of genuine dead sea salt in your anus in a sealed bag that is "highly unlikely" to break?

A life-size replica of the head of Louis Gossett Jr.?

WHAT'S YOUR PRICE!?

The Price of Discipline

Would you... limit yourself to taking 500 steps per day for a year for $10,000? How about 50 steps per day for a year for $500,000?

Would you... limit yourself to speaking 500 words per day for one week for $2,000? 50 words per day for $10,000? If at each word under 1,000 you would receive $1,000, how many words would you speak per day?

Would you... limit yourself to consuming 500 calories per day for one month for $10,000? 100 calories per day for one week for $50,000?

Would you... limit your TV viewing for a year to MTV for $25,000? QVC for $100,000? Which channel would require the largest payment?

WHAT'S YOUR PRICE!?

Nude to Lewd

Would you... pose naked in a magazine if someone else's face was Photoshopped onto the body?

Would you... pose naked in a magazine if your face was Photoshopped onto another person's more fit body?

Would you... be a naked body double in a hit movie for $20,000? Whose body double would you want to be?

How about a "face double" in a porno?
Go to http://wouldyourather.com/multimedia/videos and click on "Face Doubles" to see what this would be like?

WHAT'S YOUR PRICE!?

Not Too Picky

Would you... have sex with the following for $100,000?

A sheep?

A mule?

An alligator?

A walrus?

An oompa-loompa?

A Sleestak?

A three-way with an oompa-loompa and a Sleestak?

What's your price for all of the above? Go through one by one.

WHAT'S YOUR PRICE!?

All or Nothing

If you succeed, you get it all. If you fail, you get nothing!

Would you... attempt to eat 60 McDonald's Hamburgers in one hour for $10,000?

Would you... attempt to run a marathon in under three hours for $500,000 (you have one year to train)?

Would you... attempt to hold in your bowel movements for two weeks for $50,000?

Would you... attempt to masturbate to orgasm 10 times in a 24-hour period for $2,400? Using only Univison programming as fodder?

WHAT'S YOUR PRICE!?

Celebrity Potato Head—Women

The Deity is giving you some cosmetic surgery drawing from the body parts of celebrities. (If you are a man, consider if you would accept these exchanges for your significant other.)

Would you... want Jessica Biel's ass if you also had to have Barbra Streisand's nose?

Would you... want Salma Hayek's breasts if you also had Tina Turner's hair circa 1984?

Would you... want Elizabeth Hurley's face if you had to have Martin Scorsese's eyebrows?

Would you... want J-Lo's booty if you also had to have Jay Leno's chin?

Would you... want Pamela Anderson's body if you also had to have her hepatitis C?

Would you... want Angelina Jolie's lips if you had to have Barbara Walters's neck?

WHAT'S YOUR PRICE!?

Dr. 9021Deity

Would you... have a sex change operation for $1,000,000? $10,000,000? $100,000,000? A race change? A species change?

Would you... get a reverse face lift (i.e., the Brent Musberger) for $85,000?

Would you... have the fat sucked from your stomach, butt, and thighs for $100,000? Oh, one more thing: All of it is injected into your face.

Would you... have your Adam's apple enlarged threefold for $200,000?

WHAT'S YOUR PRICE!?

Cheat Sheet

If you never got caught, would you cheat on your girlfriend or wife with...

Jenna Jameson?

Jenna Fischer?

Jenna Haze?

Halle Berry?

The Olsen twins?

Adriana Lima?

All of the Victoria's Secret models at once?

The ghost of Harriet Tubman?

WHAT'S YOUR PRICE!?

Cheat Sheet

If you never got caught, would you cheat on your boyfriend/husband with...

John Mayer?

Orlando Bloom?

Harrison Ford?

Johnny Depp?

Tony Hawk?

Stephen Hawking?

All of your favorite musicians whenever you want?

Zeus?

WHAT'S YOUR PRICE!?

Bite Me!

How much would you pay a week for the following:

A personal masseuse?

A personal sherpa?

A personal butler?

A personal minstrel?

A personal blues musician?

A personal geisha?

WHAT'S YOUR PRICE!?

The Name Game 2: Electric Booglaoo

Would you... add "De" to the front of your first name for $260,000 (i.e., Frank becomes DeFrank)? Would you change the second and third syllables of your first name to "eesha" (i.e., Amy becomes Ameesha)?

Would you... drop the first letter of your name for $125,000 (i.e., Reggie becomes Eggie)? For the same money, would you drop the last letter? (i.e., Frank becomes Fran)?

Would you... change your first name to Funkalicious for $125,000?

Would you... insert a silent "b" in your name wherever you want for $6,500? Where would you insert it?

WHAT'S YOUR PRICE!?

Nuptials Schmuptials

The Deity moonlights as a wedding planner in order to offer an alternative to those ridiculous dominant gay guys on those wedding shows. Is he better? Well, the price is right.

Would you... battle-rap your vows for $25,000?

Would you... for $200,000, hold your wedding in a slaughterhouse? At Putt-Putt? At Office Depot?

Would you... for $12,000, replace the "you may kiss the bride" tradition with "you may grope the bride"?

How much would you pay for the Pope to be your guest minister? The guy who narrates movie trailers? Sam Perkins? The team of Sam Perkins and the Pope?

Would you... accept H.R. Pufnstuf as your best man?

A pack of Ewoks as groomsmen?

WHAT'S YOUR PRICE!?

More Punching Your Grandmother Questions

Would you... wearing a mask, punch your grandmother as hard as you can in the gut once for $700,000 if she never found out it was you?

The front of the neck?

The back of the knee?

The small of the back?

Where would you punch her if you had to choose three spots?

WHAT'S YOUR PRICE!?

The Price of Pain

Would you... let Sidney Crosby take a slapshot into your sternum for $10,000? $100,000? How about into your mouth?

Would you... light your hair on fire for five seconds for $5,000? $10,000?

Would you... light your hair on fire for thirty seconds for $300,000? How many seconds for how many dollars? How about your pubic hair?

Would you... dip your feet into a deep fryer for $25,000? Dunk your face for $250,000? Submerge your balls for $500,000 (men)? Submerge and then bite off your nipples for $5,000,000 (women)?

Would you... sit in a bathtub with a single piranha for $2,000? Twenty piranhas for $50,000? Two hundred piranhas and Art Monk for $1,000,000?

WHAT'S YOUR PRICE!?

Good Parenting

These are the circumstances: The Deity has decided to help you rear your child. You may question his technique—after all, he's operating for reasons beyond your understanding.

Would you rather have the entertainment at your child's birthday party be...

Tony Robbins *OR* Richard Simmons?

Charles Bukowski *OR* Jerry Falwell?

50 Cent *OR* Betty Big Ones?

WHAT'S YOUR PRICE!?

Life and Death

Would you... give up one year of your life for $100,000? $1,000,000? How many years would you give up for what price?

Would you... give up one year of your spouse's life for $300,000? How many years would you give up for your spouse and for what price, you greedy bastard? How about your child's life? Think of the life you could give him/her.

Would you... remain 17 years old for 20 years if when those 20 years were up you'd suddenly be 75? Would you remain 28 for 30 years if when those years were up you'd be 90? How old would you want to be for how long?

Would you... play jai-alai with Danny Glover for $19?

WHAT'S YOUR PRICE!?

Putting the "Fun" Back in Funeral

For $100,000 given to your family...

Would you... have a Viking funeral?

Would you... be buried in your backyard (and not buried very well)?

Would you... have engraved on your grave stone "Me Chinese, me play joke, me go pee-pee in your Coke"?

Would you... have an open-casket funeral where people can sledgehammer you like an old car to raise additional thousands of dollars for charity?

WHAT'S YOUR PRICE!?

Chapter Ten

Would You Rather Live in a World Where...

The world don't move to the beat of just one drum.
What might be right for you, might not be right for some.
— Ralph Waldo Emerson

God created the Earth in six days and rested on the seventh. Suffice to say, he rushed it. He put the project off to the last minute and crammed, and the sloppy work is evident everywhere: traffic, floods, the platypus, Ann Coulter. The Deity, in his pagan splendor, is going to make a few changes, and he has brought you on as a consultant.

Would you rather live in a world where...

condoms were able to magically crawl out of their wrappers and put themselves on at exactly the right moment

OR

there was a male contraceptive pill that caused some bloating and moodiness?

Would you rather live in a world where...

the moon gave out light like a disco ball

OR

where the sun was the big smiling face of Tom Bosley (Mr. Cunningham from *Happy Days*)?

Would you rather live in a world without...

TV *OR* your cousins?

Instant Messaging *OR* organized religion?

MTV *OR* PBS?

punctuation *OR* glass?

Bloggers *OR* poison ivy?

YOU MUST CHOOSE!

Would you rather...

grow up in the wild

OR

in a Sbarro's?

Would you rather...

your life be one big '80's movie shopping montage

OR

one big training sequence?

Things to consider: your best friend giving you disapproving looks while you try on outfits, vast and triumphant improvement, carrying lots of shopping bags

Would you rather live in a world where...

musicians could not appear on TV or in photographs so they were judged and heralded solely on their music

OR

a world where there were no critics?

Would you rather...

live in a musical in the tone of *High School Musical*

OR

Phantom of the Opera?

YOU MUST CHOOSE!

Would you rather live in a world where...

all presidential debates were conducted via battle rap

OR

via ultimate fighting?

Would you rather live in a world where...

all conversation was sung like in a Broadway musical

OR

sexual encounters occurred as they do in porn?

Would you rather live in a world where...

there were battle Haikus instead of battle rap:

> *Your words are so weak*
> *They fall like brittle bamboo*
> *Cracking to the ground*

OR

gangstas talked in Dr. Seuss language:

> *You're not a whatsit or whatchamacallit*
> *You're not the guy in the picture that came with my wallet*
> *You're not a hoosy or thingamajigga*
> *But dogg with two "g"'s , you my nigga!*

YOU MUST CHOOSE!

Would you rather...

live in Ancient Egypt

OR

be unable to leave the set of the Ellen DeGeneres show?

Would you rather live in a world...

where Teletubbies were a common species of creature that lived in the wild

OR

where there were evil "Bizarro" arch-enemy versions of ourselves?

Things to consider: hunting

Would you rather live in a world...

where the convention of singing "Happy Birthday" was replaced with "You Ain't Seen Nothin' Yet" by Bachman Turner Overdrive

OR

where the Pledge of Allegiance was replaced with the lyrics to "Baby Got Back"?

Would you rather live in the world of...

The Flintstones **OR** *The Jetsons*?

Narnia **OR** Middle Earth?

King of the Hill **OR** *Benny Hill*?

YOU MUST CHOOSE!

204

Would you rather...

LIVE IN A WORLD WHERE IT RAINED SUPERBALLS

OR

WHERE PEOPLE HAD MR. POTATO HEAD-STYLE FACIAL FEATURES THAT COULD BE REMOVED AND EXCHANGED?

Would you rather live in...

the *Star Wars* Universe *OR* Shakespeare's England?

a Jane Austen novel *OR* the neighborhood with the *Fat Albert* gang?

Biblical times *OR* in the world of Atari's Centipede?

Would you rather live in...

Kaiser-ruled Germany *OR* Pre-Dorothian *Oz*?

Colonial Williamsburg *OR* the recreated Colonial Williamsburg?

Tsarist Russia *OR* Czarist Russia?

Would you rather live in a world where...

genitals tasted like candy

OR

a drum set appears at the moment of orgasm so that you may better express your ecstasy?

Would you rather live in a world where...

there was no such thing as pain, but also no such thing as sports

OR

there was no such thing as world hunger, but also no such thing as Jm J. Bullock?

YOU MUST CHOOSE!

Would you rather...

LIVE IN A WORLD WHERE GOLF COURSES AND CEMETERIES WERE COMBINED ON ONE PROPERTY

OR

CHURCHES AND PAINTBALL PARKS WERE?

Would you rather live in a world where...

women were given equal pay, opportunity, and access to jobs

OR

men experience the pains of the birth process along with women?

Would you rather live in a world comprised entirely of...

Nerf *OR* Tootsie Roll?

flannel *OR* wicker?

ice-cream *OR* Alan Alda?

Would you rather live in a world painted by...

Van Gogh *OR* Seurat?

Monet *OR* Manet?

Bosch *OR* Boesch?

Would you rather live in a world where...

evolution worked in reverse

OR

it was accelerated 1,000,000 times the current rate?

YOU MUST CHOOSE!

You are stranded on a desert island.

Would you rather have...

a bottle of Scope mouthwash **OR** a bottle of Jack Daniels?

a manicurist **OR** a donkey?

a slice of veal roast **OR** a poster of the 1984 Houston Rockets?

a box of Grape-Nuts, a wrench, and a pair of fuzzy dice **OR** a jar of Vaseline, a fake moustache, and a photograph of Spiro Agnew?

Would you rather live in a world where...

marijuana was legal

OR

referring to yourself in the third person was illegal?

Would you rather live in a world where...

a bell rang to indicate when people began to bullshit

OR

every day people woke up with a completely new appearance?

YOU MUST CHOOSE!

Would you rather live in a world without...

skin moisturizer *OR* cream cheese?

Sinbad *OR* Eskimos?

Men without Hats' "Safety Dance" *OR* salmon?

David Copperfield *OR* oatmeal?

Would you rather live in a world where...

people's desired personal space was 3 inches

OR

15 feet?

Would you rather live in a world where...

Underoos were standard business attire

OR

upon meeting, humans sniffed each other like dogs?

Would you rather live in a world where...

corporate hold music was phone sex

OR

Casual Friday was preceded by Thong Thursday?

YOU MUST CHOOSE!

Workin' for the Man

The Deity has just finished a hostile takeover of your work place and he's changing the place up a bit. Schooled in the art of effective management, he's seeking employee input.

Would you rather work at a company where...

you are given great health benefits

OR

Tuesday is "No Pants" day?

Would you rather work at a company where...

the dress code is prom wear from the 1970s

OR

your boss conveys your end-of-the-year evaluation through rap?

Would you rather...

have your Lamaze coach be Marv Albert **OR** the guy from *Police Academy* who made all those crazy sound effects?

your minister be Gallagher **OR** Andrew "Dice" Clay?

your blacksmith be Dan Rather **OR** John Stamos?

YOU MUST CHOOSE!

Would you rather be...

a crash test dummy *OR* a fluffer for animal nature documentaries?

the world's greatest rhythm gymnast *OR* the last man off the bench for the LA Clippers?

a matador with a club foot *OR* a librarian with problem flatulence?
Or the reverse?

Would you rather be...

a human mannequin that just stands there all day and models clothes in a department store

OR

a ruthless and slick Special Olympics sports agent?

Would you rather live in a world where...

the profession rabbi and professional bowler were combined into one job

OR

toll booth attendant and prop comedian were?

YOU MUST CHOOSE!

213

Would you rather...

LIVE IN THE WORLD OF SPONGEBOB SQUAREPANTS

OR

POKÉMON?

Would you rather.... for beginners:

Would you rather...

be suave and sophisticated with nice hair

OR

rotund and misshapen with rickets?

Would you rather...

have $200

OR

$45?

Would you rather...

learn the teachings of Jesus

OR

those of Timothy Busfield?

YOU MUST CHOOSE!

AUTHORS' ⟵⟶ *DEBATE*

Would you rather...

have the job of your dreams

OR

sit briefly on an omelette?

Job of your dreams—David Gomberg

Imagine going to work and being excited about it. No more grind, no more slaving away with no validation or appreciation. Getting paid for what you love to do. It will improve your mood and the rest of your life as well. You spend more than half your waking life at work, and it's vital you enjoy what you do. Few of us get that chance. You'll be happy, as will your family and friends. You will excel in all areas of your life.

Sit on an omelette—Justin Heimberg

How do you know sitting on an omelette isn't the greatest thing in the world? Have you ever tried it? Didn't think so. Guess what? Sitting on an omelette is the best thing in the world. Way better than having the job of your dreams. Until you do it, you just won't get it. So go ahead, take that dream job. Knock yourself out. I'll be at home sitting on an omelette.

YOU MUST CHOOSE!

Chapter Eleven

The *Would You Rather...?* Menu

The Deity has always been a fan of the theme restaurant. His Planet 2nd Rate Hollywood was a flop with its main attractions: Judge Reinhold's half-drunken Budweiser and the Fat Guy from *Head of the Class*'s socks. But he's at it again with the *Would You Rather...?* restaurant/bar. And you are his first customer. Here's how the dinner deal works. You are given a choice between two orders. You must choose one.

Appetizers:

Would you rather eat...

a trout-shake *OR* boiled sparrow stuffed with mulch?

fried afterbirth *OR* your own left foot?

shaving scum salad *OR* a snot shot?

Would you rather eat...

200 slices of American cheese *OR* 2,000 raisins?

the contents of a full vacuum cleaner bag *OR* $45 in nickels?

ham and fudge fondue *OR* a peanut butter and whitefish sandwich?

a full stick of butter *OR* the contents of Michael Jackson's face?

From the Bar:

Would you rather drink...

a Beefbrawler (gin, orange juice, ground beef)

OR

a Bloody Pilgrim (Kool-Aid, heavy cream, a teaspoon of petrol, and mushrooms pureed to perfection)?

YOU MUST CHOOSE!

Would you rather drink...

a Retarded Beaver (gin, grenadine, cedar shavings, topped with a tuft of pubic hair)

OR

Cameron's Undoing (a jar of mayonnaise studded with pimento, garnished with a photograph of Alan Thicke)?

Would you rather drink...

Mendeleev's Apology (a dispersion of urine and paprika)

OR

a Pensive Vampire (human blood, ice, Kahlua)?

Would you rather drink...

Yellow Magic (a warm glass of melted butter seasoned with an entire shaker of salt sucked through a straw of green onion)

OR

Liz's Surprise (a mug of warm fat freshly liposucked from Elizabeth Taylor's thigh and upper arm)?

YOU MUST CHOOSE!

The Main Course:

Would you rather eat...

The Nexus
A heaping pile of umbilical cords in a blood-pesto sauce topped with tomatoes, peppers, and pancreas

OR

The Orb
Freshly baked blister filled with natural juices and stuffed to the membrane with bile?

Would you rather eat...

The Natural
Fresh roadkill (your choice of squirrel, possum, or lynx) marinated in its own (hopefully) natural juices served on a bed of fern leaves

OR

The Enigma
Nougat-covered corned beef topped with tortoise eyes, all soaked in a mysterious thick fluid?

YOU MUST CHOOSE!

Would you rather eat...

The Emperor
2 pounds of roast beef sautéed in Roger Ebert's sweat consumed to the tune of *Ride of the Valkyrie*

OR

The Regent
two charcoal briquettes on toasted roll, eaten in the presence of five surly sailors?

Would you rather eat...

The Potluck
Breaded Ray Parker Jr. on two mysterious hands garnished with the malaise of America during the Carter administration

OR

The Ennui
Pointless salad brutalized by reality punctuated with the agony that is inevitable?

YOU MUST CHOOSE!

Specials:

Guilty pleasures from the endangered species list

Would you rather eat...

Bald Eagle on a stick draped in melted Monterey Jack cheese

OR

sedated panda seasoned with its own cries of pain?

Would you rather eat...

a bowl of bat guano *OR* a mug of hot tea prepared with a used tampon?

all food in liquid form *OR* gaseous form?

salmon sorbet *OR* Dirty Coins and Cream?

baked penguin *OR* creamed Estrada?

YOU MUST CHOOSE!

223

Chapter Twelve

Wishful Thinking

The Deity has assumed corporeal form. He wears a
white suit and is flanked by a miniature Latino man,
also wearing a white suit. A plane is heard overhead,
exciting the small man to announce its arrival. Twice.
This could mean only one thing. You have arrived on
Fantasy Island. Not only do you have the chance to
fulfill a fantasy, but you get to choose between two.

Would you rather...

have a lake named after you

OR

have a popular children's multivitamin shaped in your image?

Would you rather interview...

Bill Clinton *OR* Prince?

Stephen Colbert *OR* Vladimir Putin?

J.D. Salinger *OR* J.D. Hogg?

Would you rather...

have 15 minutes of conversation with Gandhi

OR

15 minutes of unbridled passion with Katherine Heigl? Vice-versa?

YOU MUST CHOOSE!

If you could go back in time, would you rather...

dance with Fred Astaire *OR* be serenaded by Frank Sinatra?

have Leonardo Da Vinci paint your portrait *OR* have Shakespeare write you a sonnet?

have Mozart compose a symphony for you *OR* have a *Simpsons* character based on you?

Would you rather...

get drunk-dialed by Moses

OR

by Martin Luther King?

Would you rather...

bring in da noise

OR

bring in da funk?

YOU MUST CHOOSE!

Would you rather...

SEE ABRAHAM LINCOLN AND GEORGE WASHINGTON DEBATE

OR

SEE THEM PLAY A GAME OF ONE-ON-ONE BASKETBALL?

Would you rather have sex with...

Batman **OR** Superman?

The Flash **OR** Spiderman?

Toucan Sam **OR** Cap'n Crunch?

Things to consider: Cap'n Crunch's penchant for buggery

Would you rather have sex with...

The Bionic Woman **OR** Wilma from *Buck Rogers*?

Wonder Woman **OR** a real-life anatomically correct Barbie?

Snow White **OR** Rapunzel?

Things to consider: likely Rapunzel winterbush

Would you rather...

hold hands with Rod Carew

OR

catch lightning bugs with Donny Wahlberg?

YOU MUST CHOOSE!

Would you rather have your eulogy delivered by...

Barack Obama *OR* Foghorn Leghorn?

Jesse Jackson *OR* Bill O'Reilly?

Shakespeare *OR* Dr. Seuss?

The Cocoa Puffs bird *OR* the Hamburglar?

Would you rather...

be on a reality show

OR

punch everyone who has been?

Would you rather...

touch the Pope

OR

meet Bill Bellamy?

YOU MUST CHOOSE!

Would you rather spend a day with...

El DeBarge *OR* George Bernard Shaw?

Ralph Sampson *OR* Ralph Nader?

Rommel and Charles Schulz *OR* Willie Nelson and Kubla Khan?

The founding fathers *OR* the cast of *The Cannonball Run 1* and *2*?

If you were a fly on the wall, would you rather reside...

on Tom Cruise's wall *OR* on Robin Williams's?

on porn queen Jenna Jameson's wall *OR* on *Dungeons and Dragons* creator Gary Gygax's?

on Tone Loc's wall *OR* Anne Maxson's?

Would you rather spend a day with...

Paul Revere and Donny Osmond

OR

F. Scott Fitzgerald and Mr. T?

YOU MUST CHOOSE!

Would you rather...

have a mountain range named after you

OR

have a sexual position officially named after you?

Would you rather...

execute a perfect two-handed tomahawk dunk over Robert Duvall

OR

dominate Felicity Huffman in Scrabble?

Would you rather...

get drunk with Paul Bunyan

OR

Johnny Appleseed?

YOU MUST CHOOSE!

Chapter Thirteen

Mixed Blessings

The Deity's moodiness had become increasingly mercurial.
Within each option are plusses and minuses, an onslaught
of algebraic absurdity. All right, look, this chapter is a
"take it or leave it" sort of thing. Some people like the
randomness, and others think it is the dumbest thing in
the world. (Those people will be destroyed by the Deity.)

Would you rather...

look good in red but have severe problem flatulence in malt shops

OR

have a photographic memory but be compelled to perform Globetrotter-like antics with any spherical shape you come upon?

Would you rather...

have adorable dimples but be unable to hear the fourth syllable of any word

OR

have a shapely posterior but be prone to getting into fights with mannequins?

Would you rather...

be incredibly charming, but only when discussing your bowel movements

OR

have an infallible pickup line, but only with Fuddruckers employees?

Would you rather...

have the mind of William Shakespeare but the body of William Taft?

OR

the mind of Albert Einstein but the body of Fat Albert?
Things to consider: possible "Fat Einstein" cartoon

YOU MUST CHOOSE!

Would you rather...

know the times and theater locations for all movies, but have to consume all liquids by soaking/squeezing them directly into your mouth via a sponge

OR

never forget a phone number, but only be capable of seeing peripherally?

Would you rather...

never miss a bowling spare but have your upper lip nonresponsive to gravity

OR

be a masterful popsicle stick sculptor but have a contagious laugh to the point where it is a real problem?

Would you rather...

have the ability to mute the world but have George Wendt heads for feet

OR

be capable of changing your skin color to blend in with your environment but be incapable of viewing any object larger than 10 feet high?

YOU MUST CHOOSE!

Would you rather...

have pockets filled with an infinite supply of Gummi Bears but be incapable of speaking when not wearing an ascot

OR

have near-perfect knowledge of C++ programming but on Fridays become convinced you are a glass of orange juice and desperately struggle not to spill yourself?

Would you rather...

have superior cleavage-finding instincts when channel surfing but have a debilitating fear of right angles

OR

have thick lustrous hair but believe that you are Dan Aykroyd while it's light out and Pegasus while it's night?

Would you rather...

have the power to solve Rubik's cubes by putting them down your pants but only have dreams regarding anti-immigration litigation

OR

be immune to the effects of secondhand smoke but give birth to your own left foot?

YOU MUST CHOOSE!

239

Would you rather...

be found attractive by all members of the opposite sex, but secrete copious amounts of steak sauce when aroused

OR

have genitals that permanently taste like chocolate, but have all your offspring be exact clones of Walter Matthau?

Would you rather...

be a brilliant essayist but have to wear a matching set of wristbands and headband at all times

OR

have heightened Stratego intuition, but talk like Liberace when asked to repeat yourself?

Would you rather...

look respectable in sweatpants but articulate all your thoughts aloud

OR

have a great short game in golf, but compulsively fondle yourself when the doorbell rings?

YOU MUST CHOOSE!

Would you rather...

have the courage of a lion but the ass of a baboon

OR

the wisdom of an owl but the head of Epstein from *Welcome Back, Kotter*?

Would you rather...

have a firm handshake but be severely lactose intolerant

OR

be loved by animals but require the signature of Cheech Marin for all your legal documents?

Would you rather...

have a knack for model train setups but have an irresistible urge to punch people named Mildred in the breast and thighs

OR

be able to make anything shiny but be unable to refrain from making the tugboat gesture and sound any time an overweight person enters a room?

YOU MUST CHOOSE!

Would you rather...

BE AN EXPERT WHITTLER BUT HAVE A HEAD OF LETTUCE PERPETUALLY ORBITING YOU

"ELI WHITNEY PATENTED THE COTTON GIN ON MARCH 14, 1794!"

OR

BE ABLE TO BAKE SUCCULENT BROWNIES BUT HAVE A VARIETY OF TOURETTES SYNDROME WHERE YOU RANDOMLY EXCLAIM FACTS ABOUT ELI WHITNEY?

Would you rather...

be an awesome winker but have earlobes that melt like candle wax when it gets hot

OR

be able to exactly gauge the amount of cream and sugar in your coffee instinctually but have to always wear a Fruit Roll-Up yarmulke?

Would you rather...

be able to jump like Dr. J. in the ABA but always have to wear those short shorts he had

OR

have the eloquence of Thomas Jefferson but have to wear colonial garb and wig?

(Nerds only)
Would you rather...

have a 3 constitution and a 15 charisma

OR

an 18 constitution and a 10 charisma?

YOU MUST CHOOSE!

Chapter Fourteen

14

MORE SEX

Would you rather have sex with...

McDreamy *OR* McSteamy?

McCain *OR* McHale?

McDonald *OR* McCheese?

Would you rather...

have your love/sex e-mails and IM's posted on CNN.com

OR

have the soundtrack to your lovemaking available as an iTunes podcast for download?

Would you rather...

have a prehensile penis

OR

a detachable scrotum (patent pending)?

YOU MUST CHOOSE!

Would you rather have sex with...

Tom Brady

OR

Webster if they exchanged heights?

Would you rather...

your G-spot be located in your esophagus

OR

on each of your fingertips? Your eyeball? Ralph Macchio's forearm?

Things to consider: typing, swallowing, looming image of avuncular Pat Morita

Would you rather...

have Troll-doll-hair for nipples

OR

pipe cleaners for pubic hair?

Would you rather...

have your genitalia located on the palm of your left hand *OR* the front of your neck?

on the middle of your back *OR* on your elbow?

on your hip *OR* your ankle?

Things to consider: oral sex, masturbation, tailoring bills

YOU MUST CHOOSE!

Would you rather...

have testicles with the density of hydrogen

OR

testicles at three times their current density?

Things to consider: scrotum stretching

Would you rather...

regularly prematurely ejaculate by two minutes

OR

regularly prematurely ejaculate by two weeks?

Would you rather have breast implants made of...

attracting magnets *OR* repelling magnets?

immortal lightning bugs *OR* throbbing hearts?

brie cheese *OR* the spirit of Malcolm X?

Would you rather...

turn into Rip Taylor when masturbating

OR

have your sexual appetite vary directly with proximity to Radio Shack?

YOU MUST CHOOSE!

Would you rather...

have to use condoms that come in a wrapper where you have to finish the crossword puzzle before they can be opened

OR

be unable to shake the image of Meadowlark Lemon during all sexual congress?

Would you rather...

have a penis that sheds skin like a snake every week

OR

a penis that makes the sound of a rain stick when it moves?

Would you rather...

acquire all the knowledge of people you have sex with

OR

right before you climax, have the choice to store up orgasms to experience later, like the "downloading later" function on e-mail?

Things to consider: rainy days, orgasm breaks at work, nerd banging

Would you rather...

have sex with a soft and gentle Tom Brokaw

OR

a fast and furious monchichi?

YOU MUST CHOOSE!

Would you rather...

ADMINISTER ORAL SEX TO THE PHILLIE PHANATIC

OR

DRYHUMP COUNT CHOCULA?

Would you rather use as sex toys...

a wooden duck, a trident, and some balsamic vinaigrette

OR

a piano tie, a bag of croutons, a Gumby doll, and a Ronald Reagan mask?

Would you rather have sex with...

a 60% scale Jennifer Aniston *OR* a winged Kate Hudson?

Meryl Streep *OR* a jaundiced Penelope Cruz?

a three-way with Cameron Diaz and Kevin Garnett *OR* Lucy Liu and Gandalf?

Would you rather your only porn be...

John Hughes films *OR* shampoo commercials?

sex symbols of the '70s *OR* of the '50s and '60s?

video game vixens *OR* imprecise memories of Deborah Norville circa 1985?

MythBusters' experiments *OR* NBA box scores?

Would you rather...

have genital warts that resemble Lego-man heads

OR

a case of VD that causes you to pee 120-degree urine?

YOU MUST CHOOSE!

Would you rather...

have sex with a woman with Dr. Ruth Westheimer's body on the top half and Adriana Lima's body on the bottom half

OR

Adriana Lima's body on top and Grimace's body on the bottom?

Would you rather...

during sex, be able to read the mind of the person you are having sex with

OR

be able to hit yours or your partner's G-spot by finding Waldo in a *Where's Waldo* book? (Each page can be used once.)

Would you rather...

have sex with Velma from *Scooby-Doo*?

OR

Ms. Pacman?

Things to consider: orgasmic exclamations of "Jinkies!," insatiable appetite, Clyde

Would you rather...

have sex with Hugh Jackman and get the mumps

OR

have sex with John Madden and get a $200 gift certificate to JCPenney?

YOU MUST CHOOSE!

Would you rather...

HAVE SEX WITH A "10"

FIVE "2"S?

Would you rather...

have sex with Carmen Electra and lose a finger

OR

have sex with Diane Keaton and gain permanent immunity from speeding tickets?

Would you rather only be able to have sex while playing...

"Eye of the Tiger" *OR* "Beethoven's Ninth"?

Buffalo Springfield's "Stop, Hey, What's That Sound" *OR* "Hava Nagila"?

"The Wheels on the Bus Go Round and Round" *OR* William Hung's rendition of "She Bangs"?

The *Star Trek* theme *OR* the *Schindler's List* theme?

an audio book of *Angela's Ashes* *OR* recordings of a senile man trying to find his way out of a K-Mart?

Would you rather...

have your computer desktop wallpaper be a picture of a naked Warren Sapp

OR

have to always use the IM screen name "BallsMcGee," (including in professional situations)?

YOU MUST CHOOSE!

Would you rather...

have a neurological abnormality that causes you to appeal victoriously to an imaginary crowd à la Hulk Hogan after sex

OR

have a condition where as soon as you see someone take their clothes off, you point to the "appropriate" body parts and say quite suavely, "milk, milk, lemonade, 'round the corner fudge is made"?

Would you rather...

every hour on the hour, change which gender you are attracted to

OR

turn your sexual partner into Tony Danza when you climax and then turn them back to themselves the next time you have sex with them?

Things to consider: maintaining a marriage, determining who the boss is

Would you rather...

utter all exclamations during sex in Yiddish *OR* Chinese?

in sign language *OR* in the form of a question as if on *Jeopardy*?

in Pig Latin *OR* with IM acronyms?

Things to consider: rabgay hattay itttaytay; lol, brb, ftp, diithbh, ccr, elo, bto

YOU MUST CHOOSE!

Would you rather...

AFTER A NIGHT OF DRUNKENNESS, WOULD YOU RATHER... WAKE UP NEXT TO YOUR FRIEND'S WIFE

OR

CHUCK E CHEESE?

256

Would you rather...

ejaculate a deadly dart

OR

die if you are not having sex at 3:37 pm every day?

Things to consider: moving to Vegas, pulling out, work as a spy

Would you rather...

have dreadlocked pubes

OR

have nipple-itis (constant visibly erect nipples that show through anything you wear)?

Things to considers: tuxedoes, the beach, short shorts

Would you rather have sex with...

a 400-pound person on top

OR

a 300-pound person on crack?

Would you rather...

have pornographic pop-up ads constantly appearing in your thoughts

OR

have your cell phone wired into your body with the ring function set on "orgasm"?

YOU MUST CHOOSE!

Would you rather...

lactate dental floss

OR

Milwaukee's Best?

Would you rather...

watch *Girls Gone Wild*

OR

Rabbis Gone Wild?

Would you rather...

have your entire sexual history be reenacted by the animatronic robots in a Disney World ride á la the *Pirates of the Caribbean*?

OR

have the moments and characters in your sex life released by the Franklin Mint as a series of collectible porcelain figurines?

Would you rather...

tag on the phrase "for a girl" to every compliment you give a female

OR

tag on a sarcastic "Sherlock" to every sexual exclamation you utter?

YOU MUST CHOOSE!

259

Would you rather...

have your mom have to put on your condoms like she was dressing you as a child for the winter

OR

never be able to call your spouse by the same name twice?

Things to consider: coming up with new terms of endearment—Honey, Baby, Schnookeylups, Porko, Flartran, Sweetballs, Fatooshk

Would you rather your pimp be...

Strom Thurmond **OR** Emmanuel Lewis?

Grimace **OR** Chewbacca?

Vijay Singh **OR** Beetle Bailey?

Pick Your Scrotum!
Would you rather have...

a scrotum slightly too small for your testicles **OR** a scrotum that was 40 times bigger than it is currently? (testicles remain the same size)

a transparent scrotum **OR** a denim scrotum?

a pendulum scrotum **OR** a bungee-scrotum™* ?

*patent pending

YOU MUST CHOOSE!

Date, Marry, or Screw?

Here's an oldie but a goodie. We give you three names. You decide which one you'd marry, which you'd date, and which you'd screw.

Bill Clinton, George W. Bush, George H. W. Bush

Alec Baldwin, Stephen Baldwin, Daniel Baldwin

Michael Jackson circa *Thriller*, Michael Jackson circa *Bad*, Michael Jackson now

Britney Spears, Jessica Simpson, Mariah Carey

Condoleezza Rice, Connie Chung, the hot Hooters waitress with low self-esteem

YOU MUST CHOOSE!

Date, Marry, Screw, Play Ping-Pong Against, or Create a Revolutionary Movement With?

OK, you mastered that one. Now to challenge you, we've added a few more options and names, resulting in more permutations. Here you must decide, which name you'd marry, which you'd date, which you'd screw, which you'd play ping-pong against, and which you would start a revolutionary movement with.

Ben Affleck, Matt Damon, Che Guevara, ping-pong champion John Hu, Mel Gibson

Tommy Lee, Ben Franklin, Tim Duncan, The Rock, Alan Greenspan

Courtney Cox, Lisa Kudrow, Jennifer Aniston, Deborah Messing, your mother

Al Sharpton, Corey Feldman, Corey Haim, Venus Williams, the girl at Starbucks who looks a little like Larry Bird

Date, Marry, Screw, Discuss the War of 1812 With, Accompany to Six Flags Amusement Park, or Collaborate to Write Hip-Hop Album?

Jerome Bettis, Molly Ringwald, George Stephanopoulos, Eminem, Menudo, God

UN Ambassador John Boland, 50 Cent, Tiger Woods, The Teletubbies, Patrick Swayze, Roberto Benigni

Maria Shriver, Bill Wennington, Darth Maul, Hitler, a can of tennis balls, Gomberg

YOU MUST CHOOSE!

263

Would you rather use as sex toys...

a tetherball, a map of Uruguay, and a menorah

OR

some measuring spoons, a thermos, and a copy of *Old Yeller*?

You live with a roommate. You decide to use a blacklight to check your room for hidden "stains."

Would you rather find stains all over...

your washcloth *OR* your favorite cereal bowl?

your computer keyboard and mouse *OR* a framed photo of your family?

a copy of James Madison's autobiography *OR* a copy of
Would You Rather...? Overstuffed?

Would you rather have sex with...

The Tin Man *OR* The Scarecrow?

Mr. Belding *OR* Matlock?

your dentist *OR* your third grade PE teacher?

Skeletor *OR* Gargamel?

YOU MUST CHOOSE!

Would you rather...

be bisexually attracted to men and fish

OR

trisexually attracted to the opposite sex, women, and boxes of Milk Duds?

Would you rather...

be required to file an official request with the federal government in order to receive oral sex

OR

have "total number of sexual partners" be a required box to fill out on every job application?

Would you rather...

have sex with a woman that has the body of Janet Reno and the face of Angelina Jolie

OR

the body of Angelina Jolie and the face of former Milwaukee Buck Jack Sikma?
Things to consider: doggie-style

YOU MUST CHOOSE!

Would you rather have phone sex with...

Dr. Laura Schlessinger *OR* Martha Stewart?

Barbara Bush *OR* Hillary Clinton?

Things to consider: Barbara Bush has a mouth like a sailor

Barbra Streisand *OR* the ghost of Harriet Tubman?

someone who constantly corrects your grammar *OR* someone prone to quoting Joseph Goebbels throughout?

Gary Gnu *OR* Pegasus?

Would you rather your only means of birth control be...

gum *OR* an English muffin?

a rubber band and a box of Tic-Tacs *OR* a roll of "Jazz Icon" postage stamps?

a waffle cone *OR* anal sex?

a stapler *OR* an 8"x10" photograph of Wilfred Brimley?

Would you rather...

have sex with Tom Brady and get herpes

OR

have sex with Brian Williams and get a sensible but stylish tote bag?

YOU MUST CHOOSE!

Would you rather have...

9-inch nipples **OR** a 9-inch clitoris?

a 24-month menstrual cycle **OR** a 24-hour menstrual cycle?

a 4-pound tongue **OR** a 4-pound testicle?

Would you rather...

always have to have sex to Arab prayer music **OR** ragtime music?

"Oklahoma" **OR** "Swing Low, Sweet Chariot"?

The Lone Ranger Theme **OR** "Wipeout"?

"99 Red Balloons" **OR** "99 Luftballons"?

vocabulary builder CD's **OR** a loop of Louis Gosset Jr. coughing?

Would you rather...

have sex with Jenna Jameson and get crabs

OR

have sex with Katie Couric and get a nice pair of business-casual wrinkle-free slacks with solid craftsmanship?

YOU MUST CHOOSE!

Would you rather...

experience orgasm any time one of your parents does

OR

any time one of your children does?

Things to consider: life at the office, bar-mitzvahs, special pants, porn career

Would you rather have a vagina...

that acts as a guillotine one out of every eight times an object is inserted *OR* one that secretes sulfuric acid upon orgasm?

that doubles as a trash compactor *OR* a cassette player?

that howls like a wolf when the moon is full *OR* one that belts out the lyrics to Sinatra tunes on command?

Would you rather...

get punched hard in the gut by the person on your left

OR

kissed passionately by the person on your right?

YOU MUST CHOOSE!

Ménage á Troiseses
Would you rather have a three-way with...

Flavor Flav and Teri Hatcher *OR* Mitt Romney and Kelly Ripa?

Jennifer Connelly and Lawrence Taylor *OR* Jennifer Garner and Nelson Mandela?

the Olsen twins *OR* the Wonder Twins?

the *Guinness Book of Records* World's Fattest Twins (the ones who are always shown on motorcycles) *OR* the *Guinness Book of Records* World's Tallest Man and World's Shortest Man?

Things to consider: Note to self: Idea for TV show: The fat twins on motorcycles become motorcycle cops; also: try to make sentence with as many colons as possible

Would you rather have sex with...

a 5'2" version of Ashton Kutcher *OR* Jason Bateman if he put on 50 pounds?

a soft and tender Don Cheadle *OR* an excitingly rough Hamburglar?

Antonio Banderas without limbs *OR* Tobey Maguire with an extra one?

a chain-smoking Kofi Annan *OR* Ben Kingsley playing kazoo?

YOU MUST CHOOSE!

Would you rather...

BE ABLE TO FLY
BUT BE AFRAID OF HEIGHTS

OR

BECOME INVISIBLE BUT BE A
COMPULSIVE MASTURBATOR?

Would you rather have sex with...

Jessica Rabbit *OR* Daphne from *Scooby Doo*?

Connie Chung *OR* a 200% enlarged Halle Berry?

Venus Williams *OR* Sheryl Crow if she spoke in the voice of an old Jewish man?

Would you rather have sex with...

Bryant Gumbel *OR* "Weird" Al Yankovic?

Alex Trebek *OR* Larry David?

Yao Ming *OR* Mini-me from *Austin Powers*?

Johnny Depp without a leg *OR* Tom Selleck without a moustache?

Matt Damon *OR* Ben Affleck?

Matt Damon *OR* Ben Affleck if they exchanged heights?

During sex, would you rather...

utter all exclamations in the computerized voice of Stephen Hawking

OR

compulsively compliment yourself?

YOU MUST CHOOSE!

Pornification

By Andrew Benjamin

Pornographers are quick to capitalize on the success of mainstream movies. All it takes to turn an actual movie into a pornographic film is a slight tweak of the title. This process is called "pornification." For example, *Good Will Hunting*, when pornified, becomes *Good Will Humping*. Similarly, *The Terminator* becomes, of course, *The Sperminator*. For every legit movie, there exists (at least theoretically) a porn version of that movie.

Test your understanding of pornification with our Pornification Quiz. (Answers follow the quiz.) For more pornification, check out the book of the same name published by Falls Media.

Here are some pornified titles. Can you figure out the original Hollywood film that inspired them?

1. *American Booty*
2. *Titty Lickers*
3. *Grinding Nemo*

Now, the fun part. We give you the popular movie title. Can you pornify it?

4. *The Nutty Professor*
5. *S.W.A.T.*
6. *Toy Story*

YOU MUST CHOOSE!

7. *Big Trouble in Little China*

8. *Analyze This*

9. *Glory*

10. *Space Jam*

11. *Malcolm X*

12. *Chitty Chitty Bang Bang*

13. *Shaft*

14. *Cold Mountain*

15. *Lou Dobbs Moneyline*

Answers to Pornification
1) *American Beauty* 2) *City Slickers* 3) *Finding Nemo*
4) *The Slutty Professor* 5) *T.W.A.T* 6) *Sex Toy Story* or *Boy Story*
7) *Big Trouble in Little Vagina* 8) *Analize This*
9) *Glory Hole* 10) *Face Jam* 11) *Malcolm XXX*
12) *Titty Titty Gang Bang* 13) *Shaft* 14) *Cold Mountin'*
15) *Lou Dobbs Money Shot*

YOU MUST CHOOSE!

Would you rather...

be able to have sex exclusively with palindromes

OR

with people with names that start with the letter "Z"?

Things to consider: Lil, Anna, Otto, race car

During sex, would you rather hear...

"Uh-oh" *OR* "What is that?!"?

"Oops" *OR* "That's where that is"?

"Oy vey" *OR* "Circuit malfunction"?

Would you rather have phone sex with...

the narrator of all those movie trailers *OR* Alf?

Randy Jackson *OR* Donald Trump?

Dr. Seuss *OR* Bob Ross (the calm "Happy Trees" painter from PBS)?

Would you rather have sex with...

Russell Crowe *OR* Pierce Brosnan?

Clive Owen *OR* Christian Bale?

Clay Aiken *OR* Ruben Studdard?

YOU MUST CHOOSE!

Would you rather have sex with...

Gwen Stefani *OR* Jennifer Aniston?

Cameron Diaz *OR* Jennifer Love Hewitt?

the new Daisy Duke (Jessica Simpson) *OR* classic Daisy Duke (Catherine Bach)?

Rebecca Romijn *OR* Rebecca Romijn-Stamos?

Would you rather have... (women, read the following questions as "have a partner with")

a two-pronged penis *OR* a penis that bends at a right angle in the middle?

a penis that turns green and tears out of your clothing like the Incredible Hulk every time you get aroused *OR* an invisible penis?

a Rubik's Snake penis *OR* a penis that can act as a light saber upon your command?

Would you rather...

have a lover who is 6' tall with a 2-inch penis

OR

4' tall with a 12-inch penis? 3'tall with a 16-inch penis?
2' tall with a 26-inch penis?

YOU MUST CHOOSE!

Would you rather...

DATE A
HALF WOMAN/HALF HORSE

HALF WOMAN/HALF COUCH?

Would you rather...

have orgasms that feel like a brain-freeze

OR

be able to maintain an erection (men)/reach orgasm (women) only by accurately reciting the digits of Pi (you have to start over if you mess up)?
Things to consider:

3.141592653589793238462643383279502884197169399375105820974944592307816406286208998628034825342117067982148086513282306647093844609550582231725359408128481117450284102701938521105559644622948954930381964428810975665933446128475648233786783165271201909145648566923460348610454326648213393607260249141273724587006606315588174881520920962829254091715363678925903...

The Deity has always been one to fuel sibling rivalry.
Would you rather have sex with...

Alec *OR* Billy Baldwin?

Fred *OR* Ben Savage?

Orville *OR* Wilbur Wright?

Things to consider: Wilbur was hung like a Shetland pony.

Would you rather...

see an opera based on your love life

OR

a porno based on your sex life?

YOU MUST CHOOSE!

Would you rather...

ejaculate Scope *OR* Tabasco sauce?

air-rifle BB's *OR* baseball-umpire strike and ball calls?

through your nostrils *OR* through your eyes?

Would you rather have a lover with measurements...

36-26-36 *OR* 33-23-34?

44-28-40 *OR* 34-18-30?

36-52-27 *OR* 54-8-26?

8-66-84 *OR* 114-75-12?

100-100-100 *OR* 36-24-36-26-58?

5-286-3 *OR* 38-26-44 (not necessarily in that order; measurements constantly shift)?

Would you rather...

be able to have sex only on bumper pool tables

OR

in the bed of a relative?

YOU MUST CHOOSE!

Would you rather...

NEVER HAVE SEX AGAIN

OR

HAVE SEX ONCE WITH A WALRUS?

Would you rather...

have your sexual partner suddenly transported to New Orleans upon your achieving climax

OR

have your sexual exploits narrated and commented upon by the bodiless voices of Al Michaels and John Madden?

Things to consider: one-night stands, spite sex, Michaels and Madden's charming rapport

Would you rather...

receive a Cleveland Steamer from Pat Sajak

OR

a Dirty Sanchez from Dirk Nowitzki?

Would you rather have sex with...

Gwyneth Paltrow *OR* Maria Miller with a unibrow?

an albino Eva Longoria *OR* Katie Holmes slathered in mayo?

Lindsay Lohan 30 years from now *OR* Lindsay Lohan 10 years ago?

Would you rather...

have sex with Paris Hilton

OR

slap her in the face?

YOU MUST CHOOSE!

Would you rather...

HAVE A SCROTUM THAT PUFFS UP LIKE A CAR AIR BAG WHEN YOU GET SCARED

OR

A BEAT-BOXING ANUS?

Would you rather have sex with...
Ernie
OR
Bert?

Pro Bert—Justin Heimberg
Bert is a take-charge kind of guy. Ernie is submissive and inept at everything he does. He mistook a washtub for a hat. What makes you think he knows his way around a woman? Ernie is a giggly best friend, a sidekick. Bert is a romantic leading man. Bert is the strong, silent type: tall, yellow, and handsome. Plus, he's hung like a horse.

Pro Ernie—David Gomberg
When making this decision, one has to consider who would be more attentive to the needs of a woman. And clearly, the answer to this is Ernie. Ernie is one to please. Witness the dynamic between him and the more uptight Bert. Bert is high-maintenance. Bert is jaundiced. Bert is the kind of guy who would roll over and go to sleep. Ernie would cuddle with you. Ernie would tenderly sing you to sleep in his arms: "Rubber Ducky... you're the one... ."

YOU MUST CHOOSE!

Chapter Fifteen

Getting Personal

It's your turn to play deity. Challenge your friends with these personalizable dilemmas.

Would you rather...

call up (insert set of friend's parents), state your name, and have phone sex

OR

dry hump (insert somebody else's parents)?

Would you rather...

have oral sex with (insert unappealing acquaintance)

OR

lose your (insert body part)?

Would you rather...

watch (insert two unattractive acquaintances) have sex

OR

get a lap dance from (insert friend's parent)?

Would you rather...

share an 18-hour car ride with (insert annoying acquaintance)

OR

put on (insert friend)'s socks every day for a month?

YOU MUST CHOOSE!

Would you...

have sex with (insert someone repulsive) to have sex with (insert someone desirable)?

Would you rather...

bathe and powder (insert disgusting acquaintance) twice a day every day for a week

OR

slap a full nelson on (insert friend's mother) for five minutes?

Would you rather...

have (insert friend or relative) pose naked until you have painted a reasonably accurate portrait

OR

meticulously moisturize, massage, and talc (insert unattractive person)?

Would you rather...

play strip poker with (insert three relatives)

OR

rub oil on every inch of (insert vile acquaintance)?

YOU MUST CHOOSE!

Would you rather...

see (insert attractive acquaintance) naked

OR

see (someone you hate) wounded?

Would you...

perform oral sex on (insert undesirable acquaintance) to have sex with (insert celebrity)?

Would you rather eat...

(insert meat)-flavored ice cream

OR

(insert vegetable)-flavored ice cream?

Would you rather...

be caught masturbating by (insert friend of the family)

OR

catch (insert friend of the family) masturbating?

YOU MUST CHOOSE!

Would you rather...

be attached to (insert someone you do not like) at the hip

OR

have to french-kiss (insert someone three times your age) every day?

Would you rather...

have to use (insert disgusting person)'s dirty clothes as a bath towel

OR

drink a cup of (insert another disgusting person)'s sweat?

Would you rather...

play (insert board game) with (insert hot celebrity)

OR

(insert verb) with a (insert adjective) (insert former San Diego Charger wide receiver)?

Would you rather...

take a tour of Vermont's covered bridges with (insert famous dictator)

OR

play Connect Four with (insert famous artist)?

YOU MUST CHOOSE!

Would you rather...

be locked up in a 5' x 8' jail cell for a month with (insert garrulous acquaintance)

OR

(insert disgusting person)?

Would you rather...

be the personal valet for (insert famous professional athlete)

OR

the personal assistant for (insert famous actor)?

Would you rather...

be submerged in a vat of (insert liquid) until you die

OR

have your limbs torn off you one at a time by the cast of (insert sitcom)?

Would you rather...

have the face of (insert actor/actress)

OR

the IQ of (insert really friggin' smart person)?

YOU MUST CHOOSE!

Would you rather...

be limited to wearing one article of clothing for the rest of your life, (insert article of clothing)

OR

eating one food, (insert food)?

Would you rather...

be wholly and debilitatingly obsessed with (insert U.S. vice-president)

OR

be just as obsessed with (insert anything)?

Would you rather...

appear as (insert cartoon character) in all photographs

OR

sound like (insert fascist dictator) on all recordings?

YOU MUST CHOOSE!

Chapter Sixteen

Technology

As the Deity continues to score the human race report card (which by now has lot of "see me" and "sloppy" on it), he is impressed with one particular category of human achievement: technological advancement. Upon further probing, however, the Deity realizes what is responsible for such a rapid rate of technological achievement: porn. Man's insatiable need to access a greater variety and quantity of pornography has resulted in broadband Internet, streaming video, high-def DVD, and numerous medical discoveries to augment the body. There must be another way toward innovation. It's time for some divine intervention.

Would you rather...

never receive another piece of e-mail spam

OR

learn that all the spam you receive is actually 100% true?

Things to consider: constant willing sex partners who are often bored; those poor suffering people from Africa with interesting syntax; ability to add inches to your penis until your penis surpasses 10 feet in length

Would you rather...

be able to "block" people like you can with e-mail senders, so that a force field would automatically keep them out of sight from you

OR

be able to "reskin" your lover at will as you would an online avatar?

Things to consider: Who would you "block"? What would you "reskin" your lover as?

Would you rather have on your instant message buddy list...

David Sedaris *OR* Donald Rumsfeld?

Nelson Mandela *OR* porn star Kobe Tai?

Jesus *OR* Steve Kerr?

YOU MUST CHOOSE!

Would you rather...

have a Blackberry whose "smart type" feature always makes racist and bigoted assumptions of what you are typing

OR

have a stuttering automated voice on your cell phone?

Would you rather...

have a retractable stylus for a pinky fingernail

OR

a computer mouse touch pad on your left nipple?

Would you rather live in the video game...

Myst **OR** *Grand Theft Auto*?

Warcraft **OR** *Madden NFL Football*?

Halo **OR** *Zelda*?

Super Mario Brothers **OR** *Elevator Action*?

Robotron **OR** *Kaboom*?

Things to consider: frenzy of movement; monotony of moving stacked water buckets back and forth

YOU MUST CHOOSE!

If you could link your brain directly to a website to mentally access all information, video, and images at all times, would you rather be linked to...

dictionary.com *OR* juggs.com?

mapquest.com *OR* cnn.com?

theonion.com *OR* popsugar.com?

Would you rather...

the only technology you can use be what you had in 1982

OR

the only clothes you can wear be what you had in 1982?

Would you rather...

have your car have a horn like that of the General Lee in *Dukes of Hazzard*?

OR

have a car with a GPS that has the voice of Harry Caray?

YOU MUST CHOOSE!

Would you rather have your cell phone ring function set on...

Sulfur emission *OR* Pinprick?

Marv Albert yelling "Yes!" *OR* incredibly realistic sounding gunshot?

Vacuum *OR* throb?

Self-righteous Bono speech *OR* maudlin nostalgia about simpler times on the fjords?

Would you rather..

see the world in Nintendo 64 graphic quality

OR

hear all conversation as if on a spotty cell phone call?

Would you rather...

grow up in a Staples office supplies store

OR

a Home Depot?

YOU MUST CHOOSE!

Would you rather...

have a toilet that bucked like a bronco

OR

a bigoted toaster oven?

Would you rather...

play *Guitar Hero* with Jimi Hendrix **OR** Slash?

Kurt Cobain **OR** John Denver?

Jimmy Page **OR** Abe Lincoln?

Would you rather be hunted down by...

Alien **OR** Predator?

Freddie Kruger **OR** Boba Fett?

An evil version of yourself **OR** an evil version of George Washington Carver?

Things to consider: peanut guns

Would you rather...

be able to play only one video game for the rest of your life: Atari's *River Raid*

OR

have your iPod play only one album: *Jock Jams 2*?

YOU MUST CHOOSE!

Would you rather...

have phone sex with the teacher from the old Charlie Brown specials

OR

have telegraph sex? (see below for example)

PHONE SEX OPERATOR: I'm so horny STOP

YOU: What are you wearing STOP

PHONE SEX OPERATOR: Nothing STOP I'm so horny STOP

YOU: Oh yeah? STOP... (silence) No, I mean, don't stop. STOP... (silence)... Shit...

Would you rather...

be able to hear every cell phone ring in your neighborhood

OR

smell every fart?

YOU MUST CHOOSE!

Sins

Sometimes circumstances make a man do evil things. Other times the Deity does. Why? That's right, reasons beyond your understanding. In any case, you must commit a horrible, terrible sin. You must turn to, shall we say, the lesser of two evils.

Would you rather...

burn down an orphanage

OR

run over a litter of newborn puppies with your lawn mower?

Would you rather...

kick your aunt in the stomach

OR

drop 200 turtles off a 40-story building?

Would you rather....

litter

OR

retransmit a baseball game without written consent from the owner?

YOU MUST CHOOSE!

Chapter Seventeen

What's Your Price...?
Part 3

Would you...

Would you... have sex with a walrus to have sex with any ten people of your choice (each person one time)?

Would you... make out with and grope feverishly your best friend's mom for 40 minutes for $150,000?

Would you... want a second portable set of "voodoo doll" genitalia that communicates all sensation to your real genitalia?
Things to consider: theft, pets, surreptitious self-pleasure

Would you... want to be able to perform oral sex on yourself?
Things to consider: never wanting to leave the house, which leads to lack of exercise, which leads to weight gain, which leads to no longer being able to continue said ability

WHAT'S YOUR PRICE!?

It Pays the Bills

Would you... mop up at peep shows for $150,000 per year?

Would you... be a high school bus driver for $100,000 a year? A high school teacher? A preschool teacher? A high school janitor?

Would you... be a human crash test dummy for $1,000,000 per accident? How many accidents would you do?

Would you... be Naomi Campbell's personal assistant for $100,000 a year? How about Tom Sizemore's assistant? Simon Cowell's?

Would you... dance at an upscale strip club called Barely Burlesque for $10,000 a week, tax-free? What about at a seedy strip club called Mufftown, USA, where they are known to throw bottle caps and lunch meat at you?

WHAT'S YOUR PRICE!?

305

What's Your Price...? Part 3

Life's a Gamble

Are you a gambler? The Deity wants to find out. Would you take part in the following coin tosses?

You Win: You have sex with anyone you want whenever you want

You Lose: You can never have sex again

You Win: You live to 250

You Lose: You die in the next 24 hours

You Win: You can eat whatever you want without gaining weight

You Lose: You can only consume insects

You Win: You get to be on the New York Yankees

You Lose: You get to be on the Baltimore Orioles

WHAT'S YOUR PRICE!?

The Price of Sacrifice

Would you... never go to a movie again for $1,000? $20,000? $100,000?

Would you... never eat cooked food again for $5,000? $50,000? $500,000?

Would you... never talk again for $500,000? $5,000,000? $25,000,000? How about if you could only talk in jive?

Would you... never have another sexual encounter for $1,000,000?

Would you... never again use the word *fabulous* for $200? *Baby* for $50,000? *Aardwolf* for $45? All adjectives for $900,000?

WHAT'S YOUR PRICE!?

Strike a Deal!
Public Restroom Etiquette

How much would you pay your friend to complete these dares:

Go over to a guy using a urinal and share it?

Stand about 6 inches too far away from a urinal than standard?

Stand about 36 inches too far (explain you're working on your range)?

Take a dump in a urinal like Randy Quaid did in the movie *Kingpin*?

For more ideas like this, check out our book MindF*cks.

$ WHAT'S YOUR PRICE!? $

Dining for Dollars

Which of the following would you eat for $1,000?

A live worm?

A calf eyeball?

This book?

A pubic hair sandwich?

A bowl of lice?

Which of the following would you eat for $40,000?

A partially developed duck embryo?

A horse rectum?

A live rat?

A rusty razor blade?

10,000 calories a day for one month (you choose the food)?

WHAT'S YOUR PRICE!?

And You Thought Algebra Was Useless

You are going to have a threesome. Mazel tov. The conditions are that your partners need to total a height of 14 feet. How do you divide the height of your partners? How do you go about your activity?

You are going to have another threesome. Mazel tov, once again. This time the weight of your partners must equal 500 pounds. How do you divide the weight? How do you go about your activity?

You are going to have a sexual free-for-all with 10 members of the opposite sex at once. Big-time mazel tov. This time the total height can equal 20 feet. How do you divide the height? How do you go about your activity?

Maximum Security

Would you... spend a day/night in a maximum security prison for $10,000 (your cellmate is in for armed robbery)?

Would you... spend a day/night in a maximum security prison for $100,000 (your cellmate is in for sexual assault)?

Would you... spend a day/night in a maximum security prison for $5,000 (your cellmate is in for impersonating Geoffrey Chaucer)?

Would you... voluntarily lock yourself up in a maximum security prison for 10 years if at the end of those 10 years you received $10,000,000? What about minimum security?

Would you... share a cell for a year with Meadowlark Lemon for $100,000?

WHAT'S YOUR PRICE!?

Manly Sports

Would you... play a game in the NFL with your talent and build without a helmet for $35,000? Without a cup for $10,000? If you got an additional $10,000 for every yard gained?

Would you... return a punt while blindfolded in an NFL game for $15,000?

Would you... go one round with Mike Tyson, in order to go one night with Carmen Electra? Two rounds for two nights? How many rounds if there is no knock-out or TKO?

Would you... get into the ring with Muhammad Ali (past) for 60 seconds for $50,000? Muhammad Ali (present day) for $500?

Would you... take a hit from a pitch by Roger Clemens for $5,000? (You're allowed to avoid the ball, if you can.)

WHAT'S YOUR PRICE!?

Personal Life

How much would you pay a week for the following:

A personal trainer?

A personal chauffeur?

A personal masseuse with a "happy ending" included?

A discreet roving personal DJ who played music to accompany your every move?

A personal S.W.A.T. team that watched your back, ready to spring into action at the first hint of danger?

A personal sorcerer? Who seems a little too attracted to you?

YOU MUST CHOOSE!

What's Your Price...? Part 3

DeitTV

The Deity is in charge of his own network and has some interesting programming in mind.

Would you... want to have a reality show based on your workplace? Your neighborhood? Your life back in high school?

Would you... pay $10,000 to see your life story on the big screen with all of the people from your life played by your favorite stars? Who would you get to play whom? What would be the soundtrack?

Would you... accept the challenge to debate your choice of Hillary Clinton, George Bush or Flavor Flav on national TV?

Would you... take $100,000 for all of your erotic dreams to play on public access TV at 3am each night?

What genre would you want a movie or TV show based on your life to be?

WHAT'S YOUR PRICE!?

The Price of Sleep

Would you... limit your sleep to four hours per day for the rest of your life to earn $250,000 per year for doing so? Three hours? Two hours? Thirty minutes?

Would you... sleep each night hanging upside down like a bat, for $500,000? For the same price, would you sleep standing up leaning against a wall? Only while in transit?

Would you... have all your dreams be silent movies for $100,000?

Would you... sleep a night in a room with an eerie but harmless live clown lurking in the corner for $1,000?

What's In a Name?

Would you... have sex with every celebrity named "Janet" to have sex with every celebrity named "Eva"?

Would you... have sex with every celebrity named "Dennis" to have sex with every celebrity named "George"?

Would you... want to have sex with every celebrity named "Tori"?

Would you rather... have sex with every celebrity named
"Jennifer" *OR* "Jenna"?
"Jessica" *OR* "Cindy"?
"Hillary" *OR* "Oprah"?

Would you rather... have sex with every celebrity named
"Ted" *OR* "Al"?
"Bruce" *OR* "Vince"?
"Jamie" *OR* "Regis"?

WHAT'S YOUR PRICE!?

Leading Ladies

How much would you pay for one steamy night with...

Jessica Simpson?

Maria Sharapova? Things to consider: grunts of passion

Natalie Portman?

Tera Patrick?

Nicole Richie anorexic?

Nicole Richie at her normal healthy weight?

Keira Knightley?

The ghost of Rosa Parks?

YOU MUST CHOOSE!

HOW MUCH?

Leading Ladies

How much would you pay for one steamy night with...

Jared Leto?

James Franco?

David Beckham?

Tom Brady?

The ghost of Pele?

Brad Pitt?

Tom Hanks?

Jon Bon Jovi?

Jay-Z?

Daniel Craig?

YOU MUST CHOOSE!

Perversion Excursion

Would you... have sex with Scarlett Johansson (men) / Josh Duhamel (women) if your foreplay had to include a Dirty Sanchez?

Would you... have sex with Heidi Klum (men)/George Clooney (women) if the sex had to include an Arabian Goggles?

Would you... have sex with your favorite model/actor if they were wearing a Nixon mask?

Would you... have sex with your celebrity crush if the sex had to include 40 minutes of "Dog in the Bathtub"?

WHAT'S YOUR PRICE!?

Minor League Baseball Team or Deviant Sex Act?

Columbus Clipper?

Toledo Mud Hen?

Cleveland Steamer?

Topeka Destroyer?

New Orleans Zephyr?

Tucson Sidewinder?

Answers: Cleveland Steamer and Topeka Destroyer are sex acts; the rest are baseball teams.

WHAT'S YOUR PRICE!?

WOULD YOU RATHER...? Overstuffed

Making Your Parents Proud

Would you slyly masturbate to the point of orgasm...

On a plane for $2,000?

At a Starbucks for $3,000?

In the audience at a Broadway show for $2,500? While performing in a Broadway show for $50,000?

During a funeral for $100,000?

While driving for $2,000?

While getting a haircut for $25,000?

WHAT'S YOUR PRICE!?

Fun With Adhesives

Would you... Krazy Glue your pinky and ring finger together for two days for $250? Your thumb, index finger, ring finger, and pinky all to your palm for $1,000? Simulate that now.

Would you... Krazy Glue your palms together for a day for $2,000? Your shoes onto your feet for $5,000? Pubic hair clippings onto your lips for $25,000?

Would you... papier-mâché your entire body (with holes to eat, see, and breathe) and leave it on for a week for $50,000?

Would you... believe that "papier-mâché" is automatically spell-checked and accented properly when you type it in Microsoft Word? Good work, Gates.

WHAT'S YOUR PRICE!?

The Price of Ink

It's time to get another tattoo. Once again, the price is what you receive for getting inked.

Your choice of a major U.S. city's subway map... $10,000?

A pocket protector and pens over left breast... $16,000?

The face of William Shatner on crotch... $50,000?

The crotch of William Shatner on face... $100,000?

The Chinese symbol for "Chinese symbol"... $1,000?

The Chinese symbol for "I'm just trying to get laid"... $11,000?

What is the weirdest tattoo you'd get? What word would you get if you had to get one word? What quote? Maybe "There are no time-outs in the world of professional wrestling." Just an idea.

WHAT'S YOUR PRICE!?

Stopwatch

Would you... watch your parents having sex for $10,000? $100,000? What's your price?

Would you... watch the long-lost Roseanne Barr/Tom Arnold sex tape for $3,000?

Would you... watch Rosie O'Donnell go to the bathroom for $1,000? Diarrhea for $2,000? Would you watch Rosie O'Donnell do anything at any time for any amount of money?

Would you... watch a stranger be eaten by a lion for $25,000? $100,000? What's your price?

WHAT'S YOUR PRICE!?

Pain, Pain, Go Away

Would you... smoke a poison oak cigarette for $20,000?

Would you... eat a four-inch-by-four-inch piece of honeycomb covered in bees for $12,000?

For $250,000, would you... swallow and pass a Rubik's Cube? An extra $500,000 if you can solve it while passing it?

Would you... let a dentist give you a root canal with no anesthesia for $10,000? $50,000?

Would you... let a proctologist give you a colonoscopy with no sedative or medication for $20,000? Would you let a dentist give you a colonoscopy and a proctologist give you a root canal for $100,000?

WHAT'S YOUR PRICE!?

Potluck

Would you... give away your life's savings to have a 100-mile-per-hour fastball?

Would you... walk with a limp for the rest of your life for $500,000? Walk with a pimp strut? A speed-walk? A moonwalk?

Would you... pay $10,000 to add one inch to your penis? $50,000? $500,000? How much would you pay per inch? How many inches would you add? Women: Read this as "Would you pay money for your spouse/boyfriend/lover to add..."

Would you... grow and sport for one year an afro with a 4-inch radius for 10,000? 8-inch radius for $50,000? 16-inch for $200,000?

Would you... allow each of your sexual partners to rate your performance in bed on the Internet for $10,000?

Give It Up!

For $10,000 deposited in your bank account today, which of the following would you give up for life?

Tomatoes?

MTV?

Gossip magazines?

Downloading music?

Watching baseball?

Smirking?

Nostalgia?

The word *very*?

Nickels?

For $100,000, which of the above would you give up?

WHAT'S YOUR PRICE!?

All or Nothing

The Deity hangs out with Michael Vick and not surprisingly likes to put on fights for show. And so these are the circumstances: Winner takes home $1,000,000, and the fight is to the death.

Would you fight...

Two Gary Colemans?

A blind gorilla?

Ryan Seacrest?

100 bullfrogs?

A ninja who is also looking for his keys at the time?

3,000 Weebles?

Three sentient beach umbrellas?

WHAT'S YOUR PRICE!?

Strike a Deal!
Street Cred

Would you... street-perform in a public place for an hour if your friends promised to match the money you made times 10 (i.e., if you make $20, they give you $200)? Choose from the following talents:

Playing the spoons

Kazoo

A one person show of *Hamlet*

Grease

A hybrid of *Hamlet* and *Grease*

Erotic dancing

Mime

Break-dancing

Tap-dancing

Ice-sculpting

Rhythmic gymnastics

Speed-chess against yourself

WHAT'S YOUR PRICE!?

Well, Pierce My Brosnan

Would you... pierce your nipples for $1,000? 10,000? What's your price? Name everywhere you'd pierce for $1,000? What's your pierce?

Would you... get a taint piercing the size of a pearl for $100,000? The size of a marble? The size of a superball? A piercing of a key ring with your keys permanently on it?

Would you... for $2,500 pierce your ear with a toothpick (you have to get all the way through)? A Capri Sun straw? A screw?

Would you... get a piercing anywhere with a working grandfather clock pendulum for $100,000? Things to consider: Why don't they have earrings with moving parts like turning gears or something? Transformer earrings? Puzzles? It's a completely untapped market.

Would you... wear cat embryo earrings for a day for $1,000? $10,000? What's your price?

WHAT'S YOUR PRICE!?

Public Knowledge

How much would you pay to have the following things made public knowledge:

Who has fake breasts and who has real breasts

Who has had any cosmetic surgery and all the details

What happens in the afterlife

What really happened with Dave Chappelle

What really happened with O.J.

How much would you pay for a daily tabloid (where the stories were sensationalized but true) about the people in your neighborhood? What if you could be tabloid fodder as well?

How much, if anything, would you pay to see an "outline" of your future (it could not be changed)? A four-page memo hitting the highlights? A treatment? A full script? A script that has been "Hollywooded" up?

YOU MUST CHOOSE!

The Sporting Life

Would you... take a charge from Shaq for $500?

Would you... take a free kick to the nuts by David Beckham for $1,000?

Would you... get drilled with a blindsided tackle by Joey Porter for $2,000?

Would you... get hit in your unprotected chest with a Mario Lemieux slapshot for $25,000 and a newfound ability to spell all French words and names?

Would you... take a croquet shot in the foot by Ernie "The Hammer" Kerchanski for $25?!

WHAT'S YOUR PRICE!?

The Price of Envy

How much would you pay to be the following for one day and why...

Guys

Bono?

Tom Brady?

Steve Carell?

David Beckham?

Hugh Heffner?

George Bush?

George Washington?

Gary Gnu?

Women

Paris Hilton?

Perez Hilton?

Laura Bush?

Kelly Clarkson?

Queen Elizabeth?

Angelina Jolie?

Cleopatra?

Mrs. Bono?

What's Your Price...? Part 3

YOU MUST CHOOSE!

Indecent Proposals

The Deity liked that movie *Indecent Proposal*. It inspired him to pose the following questions.

Would you... if your spouse agreed and there were no repercussions thereafter, let a disease-free stranger have sex with your spouse once for $1,000,000?

Would you... let this same debonair stranger dry-hump your spouse awkwardly for four minutes in a back seat of a Chevy for $60,000?
"Two minutes in the closet" for $20,000?

Would you... if she agreed, accept $1,000,000 for the same stranger to deflower your 18-year-old daughter?

What if that stranger was Dikembe Mutombo?

WHAT'S YOUR PRICE!?

Ye Olde Masturbation Page

Would you... for $400,000 give up masturbating for the rest of your life?

Would you... for $300,000 have to masturbate the rest of your life with closed fists?

Would you... for $600,000 only be able to masturbate in JCPenney stores? Radio Shacks? People named Mervin's homes?

Would you... for $700,000 masturbate the rest of your life with your feet?

Would you... never make another easy masturbation joke again for $100,000?

WHAT'S YOUR PRICE!?

Gross Price

Would you... for $2,000, fully use bath and face towels that had never been washed in the 10 years of a hotel's opening?

Would you... be thrown up on (your neck and chest while wearing a tank top) for $300?

Would you... drop an earthworm in your ear for $1,000?

Would you... consume a vomit Popsicle for $5,000? How about a Crapsicle for $50,000?

Would you... tongue clean the armpits of all the Seattle Supersonics players after each basketball game for one season for $500,000?

Would you... lick the top of an ant hill for $250?

WHAT'S YOUR PRICE!?

Meaningless

Would you... sit on a bowl of green beans for an hour for $120 dollars?

Would you... pay $60 to play one round of Boggle with Gary Sinise?

Would you... belly-flop off the low dive to understand how to correctly use the word *vouchsafe*?

Would you... take the name of your spouse upon marriage if it were "Destructo"?

Would you... like to find your true passion in life if it were throwing ladles into a river?

WHAT'S YOUR PRICE!?

Deity Boutique

Which of the following would you wear for one week straight for $1,000?

A Superman costume?

Swim goggles?

Nothing but a black leather g-string?

A sombrero?

A pirate's eye patch?

A suit made from cow fat?

A Storm Trooper costume?

Your spouse's wardrobe?

Brass knuckles?

WHAT'S YOUR PRICE!?

You're Covered

Would you... have all your toes surgically removed for $200,000? Your nipples for $100,000? How about your arms for $1,000,000? What body parts for what price?

Would you... have your eyelashes permanently removed for $200,000?

Would you... have miniature ivory elephant tusks implanted in your face for $20,000,000?

Would you... have a shark's fin added to your back for $1,000,000?

Would you... give your left nut for all the tea in China?

WHAT'S YOUR PRICE!?

Your Better Half

How well do you know your significant other?

Would he/she... blog your sex life for $1,000 a week? $10,000?

Would he/she... have a threesome with Angelina Jolie?

Would he/she... ever get any type of plastic surgery? What if it were free? And painless?

Would he/she... steal from a store if there were no chance he/she would be caught?

Would he/she... pose naked on an Internet site for $100,000?

WHAT'S YOUR PRICE!?

Strike a Deal!
Getting Personal

Would you... give a full body massage and oiling to (insert unhygienic friend) for $250?

Would you... share a weekend in Amish country with (someone you hate) for $500?

Would you... manually gratify (insert friend's relative) for $100,000?

Would you... be limited to reading (insert book title) the rest of your life for $100,000?

Would you... wrestle (insert someone else in the room with you) if the loser had to be the other's slave for a day? *Strike a deal!*

WHAT'S YOUR PRICE!?

You've Got the Power

How much would you... pay to never again have your cell phone reception go out?

How much would you... pay to always know for sure when someone is lying to you?

How much would you... pay to have the ability to see through tinted windows?

How much would you... pay to have the power to know what someone looks like just by hearing their voice?

How much would you... pay to have the power to know what someone's face looks like just by checking out their ass?

WHAT'S YOUR PRICE!?

Would You...

Would you... have sex with John Daly daily to have sex with Keira Knightley nightly?

Would you... want to be immune from all traffic laws if you had to drive a '70's style van with a moonscape and Pegasus airbrushed on the side?

Would you... share an apartment with Corey Feldman to lower your rent by $600 a month?

Would you... have sex with someone of the opposite sex who has a perfect body but has your face?

Would you... permanently chain a penguin to your leg to be able to have sex with anyone you want?

Would you... (if male) give up an inch of your height for an inch of penis size? If female, would you trade one inch of your significant other's height for an inch added to his penis size?
How many inches would you trade?

WHAT'S YOUR PRICE!?

Chapter Eighteen

Best of the Deity's Greatest Hits

Up in the heavens, the Deity is cleaning out the attic of his divine mind, a difficult task considering the brain and hair of the Deity are one organ, in which lies his power. And as he combs through his brainfro, questions are raked from its recesses and fall upon you like celestial dandruff. You cannot predict what sort of dilemma you may face, but as always, you can and must choose.

Would you rather...

walk like an 80-year-old

OR

a 2-year-old?

Would you rather...

have erasers for lips

OR

corkscrews for pinky fingernails?

Would you rather...

have sex with a 10 *OR* two 5's? (5's are at the same time)

a 10 *OR* ten 1's?

a 10 with syphilis *OR* a 4 with nice high-thread-count sheets?

Siamese twin 10's *OR* just one 10?

Would you rather...

have Confederate flag irises

OR

elliptical pupils?

YOU MUST CHOOSE!

The Deity has imprisoned you in a closed room. You are in a fight to the death. All enemies are hostile.

Would you rather fight...

a tiger with no front legs *OR* 800 bullfrogs?

3,000 butterflies *OR* one bobcat?

Lawrence Taylor *OR* the cast of the *Wonder Years*?

300 remote control cars *OR* 30 sentient red rubber playground balls?

Would you rather...

speak in the style and grammar of Biblical times

OR

conduct all written work in the voice of Snoop Dogg?

Would you rather...

have a reverse digestive tract

OR

not?

YOU MUST CHOOSE!

HAVE TO SHOWER AND BATHE DAILY WITH A HIPPOPOTAMUS (HIPPOPOTAMUS IS NOT DANGEROUS)

HAVE TO LIVE WITH FORMER NBA GREAT PATRICK EWING (EWING IS NOT DANGEROUS)?

Would you rather...

have your face on the national currency

OR

have your ass on the national currency?

Would you rather...

have sex in front of your grandparents

OR

the *American Idol* judges?

Would you rather...

menstruate Yoo-Hoo

OR

have hot fudge post-nasal drip?

Things to consider: weight gain

Would you rather...

be incapable of seeing or hearing people over the age of 40

OR

under the age of 20?

Things to consider: marriage, kids, quiet plane rides

YOU MUST CHOOSE!

Would you rather...

have your feces undulate and ooze like in a lava lamp upon falling in the toilet

OR

be able to fart Morse code?

Things to consider: rainy days, secretly relaying the truth if captured and filmed.

Would you rather...

only be able to travel downhill for the rest of your life (you get to first move anywhere you want)

OR

only be able to use words to speak in alphabetical order (each ensuing word must come later alphabetically than the one before it)?

Things to consider: Give both a try for as long as you can.

Would you rather...

swear like Chef Gordon Ramsay

OR

swear like Q*bert?

YOU MUST CHOOSE!

Would you rather...

HAVE AN AIRPLANE SEAT
NEXT TO FAT ALBERT

OR

A WOEFULLY INSECURE
SLEESTAK?

On a cross-country flight, would you rather sit next to...

a heavy breather *OR* a 2-year-old?

an unshowered hobo *OR* a Mormon missionary?

an argumentative matador *OR* Gropey McGee?

Would you rather...

use silverware pieces that are unwashed surgical instruments recently used in an open heart surgery operation

OR

use a straw that was cut from unwashed tubing used in a liposuction procedure?

Would you rather...

turn into Sammy Davis Jr. when masturbating

OR

have the AOL "you've got mail" guy announce your orgasms?

Would you rather...

emit steam from your ears when you're angry

OR

exude Tang from your hands when you're tardy?

YOU MUST CHOOSE!

Would you rather...

drink a cappuccino topped with whipped rabid St. Bernard slobber froth

OR

iced tea sweetened with a spoon of vaginal discharge from a VH1's *Rock of Love With Bret Michaels* contestant?

Things to consider: infections

Would you rather...

play 30 minutes of continuous dodgeball against Peyton Manning

OR

have a three minute slap fight with Floyd Mayweather?

Would you rather have sex with...

a bearded Paris Hilton *OR* a breaded Christina Applegate?

Glenn Close *OR* a three-times-the-normal-density Catherine Zeta Jones?

Rebecca Lobo *OR* an eight-month pregnant Elizabeth Hurley?

Would you rather...

have your tongue be twisted 720 degrees

OR

have your septum torn out with a staple remover?

YOU MUST CHOOSE!

Would you rather...

slowly insert a 3-inch needle into your navel

OR

have to stand on a fired-up BBQ grill for one minute?

Would you rather...

have to wash your face every day in a heavily populated birdbath

OR

have to always use the piece of toilet paper from the person who last used the toilet?

Would you rather...

try to walk once around on the edge at the top of the Empire State Building on a windy day

OR

headbutt a Rottweiler 10 times and see what happens?

Would you rather...

have a restless leg and a lazy eye

OR

a lazy leg and a restless eye?

YOU MUST CHOOSE!

Would you rather...

SUCK ON A
PUBIC HAIR GOBSTOPPER

OR

A FROZEN URINE POPSICLE?

If your life depended on it, would you rather...

stack five uncooked grains of rice on top of each other

OR

spin four quarters at once?

Things to consider: Try it. You have five minutes.

If your life depended on it, would you rather...

have to achieve orgasm while listening to "Follow the Yellow Brick Road"

OR

while staring (your eyes cannot close other than blinking) at a framed 8" x 10" photo of Alf?

Things to consider: Try it. You have five minutes.

Would you rather...

have an inch of flimsy extra skin at the end of your fingers like gloves that are too big

OR

react like a crying, screaming, jubilant teenage girl seeing the Beatles for the first time whenever you are introduced to a new person?

YOU MUST CHOOSE!

Would you rather...

play a game of paintball with the Dalai Lama

OR

play a round of 20 Questions with Shannon Sharpe?

Would you rather...

conclude all prayers with "Yeah, Boyeeee!" instead of "Amen"

OR

have your family solemnly recite the lyrics to the "Super Bowl Shuffle" instead of the Lord's Prayer before each meal?

Things to consider: (say with very grave tone) "We are the Bears Shufflin' Crew; Shufflin' on down, doin' it for you. We're so bad we know we're good.
Blowin' your mind like we knew we would. Yeah, Boyeeeee!"

Would you rather...

be near-sighted in one eye and far-sighted in the other (and not be allowed to wear glasses or lenses)

OR

have a rare form of amnesia where you have no recollection of anything that happens on Tuesdays?

YOU MUST CHOOSE!

Would you rather...

cough anally

OR

fart orally? Excrete ocularly?
Things to consider: getting bronchitis

(Typo-inspired)
Would you rather...

have an incurable case of head dice

OR

get a face-shift (everything pulled a little to the left)?

Would you rather...

be able to speak English but only be able to hear words that are spoken to you in Uzbek

OR

have a corneal disease that causes you not to be able to see the letter "s"?
Things to consider: translators, the Slaughterhouse

YOU MUST CHOOSE!

Would you rather...

have thorn-covered skin

OR

at parties, be unable to hold conversations about anything other than Max Headroom?

Would you rather...

have to conduct all business meetings in the *Pole Position* arcade game

OR

any time you see a baguette, have an unstoppable compulsion to wield it and smash things maniacally like Bam Bam from *The Flintstones*?

Would you rather...

every Thursday, have a Samurai sword permanently but painlessly embedded in your back, causing you to stagger around, constantly about to die, forever trying to utter your last words

OR

gradually turn your surroundings into a Panera wherever you go starting after about 15 minutes and taking about an hour to completely Panera-ize?

YOU MUST CHOOSE!

Would you rather...

have your brain put on size and weight as you learn new things

OR

have everything you say sound as if you're falling off a cliff, making your voice trail away?

Things to consider: Would you just stay dumb?

Would you rather...

have a loyal hunting falcon at your beck and call but have perpetual hat head

OR

be able to pull off wearing tights but be shamefully attracted to Dora the Explorer?

Would you rather...

be able to turn any piece of paper into a Post-it Note

OR

be able to immediately end arguments if you sneeze?

Would you rather...

be only able to see yourself through Ernest Hemingway's eyes

OR

have self-esteem dependent upon your proximity to granite quarries?

YOU MUST CHOOSE!

Would you rather...

have the ability to silence with a stare

OR

goose with a wink?

Would you rather...

be unable to understand the written word unless read to you by *Dukes of Hazzard* star Tom Wopat

OR

have your legal name changed to "Doo-Doo McGee"?
Things to consider: office staff meetings, contract signings

Would you rather...

have the peripheral vision of Magic Johnson

OR

the magic vision of Peripheral Johnson? (work in progress)

Would you rather...

have to communicate solely in baby talk

OR

in *Three's Company*-style double-entendre?

YOU MUST CHOOSE!

Would you rather...

have breasts that age 10 times faster than the rest of your body

OR

have a neck that gains weight 10 times faster than the rest of your body?

Would you rather...

have four knuckle fingers, pronounce every third word "kelbor," be allergic to Don Mattingly, and have a breeze that perpetually blows by making your hair look healthy and manageable like models'

OR

have to play all sports holding hands with Tim McGraw, speak like an 18th-century British dowager, be shrouded in fog, age to 40 then reverse, and always feel like you do when you bite into an ice-cold popsicle with your most sensitive teeth?

Would you rather...

see the world in Atari 2600 graphic quality

OR

only be able to use four words: *lozenge*, *kelp*, *vindication*, and *wheelbarrow*?

YOU MUST CHOOSE!

Would you rather...

BE LIMITED TO CLEANSING YOURSELF BY USE OF A DUSTBUSTER

OR

HAVE HAIR THAT CHANGES COLOR AND FALLS OUT IN THE AUTUMN?

Would you rather...

be incapable of moving your body once sexually turned on

OR

be completely infertile/impotent except when inside churches?

You have just been hired by the head of the PGA to change one rule.

Would you rather...

allow loud heckling at greens

OR

have quicksand traps?

As NBA commissioner,

Would you rather institute...

a two-second shot clock

OR

a three-feet-tall maximum height rule?

You have been appointed baseball commissioner.

Would you rather...

put spikes on the outfield wall at baseball games

OR

light the bases on fire?

YOU MUST CHOOSE!

You have just become boxing commissioner.

Would you rather...

limit punching to below the belt

OR

have tag-team matches?

Would you rather...

perpetually feel like you're walking through cobwebs

OR

have sandy insides?

Would you rather...

perpetually feel the annoyance and embarrassment you experience when they sing "Happy Birthday" to you at a crowded restaurant

OR

the frustration of the 15th minute looking for your keys?

Would you rather...

walk like an Egyptian

OR

date a girl with an unwavering propensity to party all the time?

YOU MUST CHOOSE!

Would you rather...

BE STUCK ON AN ELEVATOR WITH AVID JEHOVAH'S WITNESS MISSIONARIES

OR

FLATULENT SUPERMODELS?

Would you rather...

wake up each day with a completely new face

OR

a completely different age?

Would you rather...

use an inhaler of crushed poison ivy

OR

receive acupuncture with a nail gun?

Would you rather...

speak like a retarded Elvis

OR

speak like a super-sarcastic JFK?

Would you rather never be able to use...

toilet paper *OR* the letter "e"?

shampoo *OR* profanity?

shoes *OR* any verb other than "destroy"?

YOU MUST CHOOSE!

Would you rather read...

Girls Gone Wild: The Novel

OR

Donkey Kong: The Novel? (See below.)

-1-

   She pried off the water-saturated mini-T-shirt, the last obstinate cling releasing like the inhibition she was shedding.

   "Whoooo-hooooo yeahhhh" bellowed the crowd who below her awaited their daily feeding of lascivious images like seals at Sea World.

   "Whooo-hoo, yeahhhhh!" confirmed a posse of drunken members of the Kappa Sig fraternity who teetered on a balcony across the parade-laden street.

   Spurred by the wanton courage of her compatriot, the young lady's peer delicately lifted her shirt, exposing part of one breast, as if she were grinning wryly, and then quickly let the shirt recede to gravity's will.

   "Seniors '05!" proffered a young man with vomit crusted on the corner of his mouth.

   "Whoooo Yeahhhhhhhh!" his friend added.

YOU MUST CHOOSE!

-2-

He leaped with all his might over the rolling barrel, fighting to keep his eyes forward and not lift his gaze toward the captive damsel. The hammer hovering mere inches away, it was time to turn the tables. With a last vestige of energy, Mario grasped for the hammer and seized it with the determination of a plumber who had a problem to fix.

"Oh, if my brother Luigi, could see me now," thought the mustachioed stereotype. BAM! The barrel was no match for the mighty swing of the stout and proud Italian. BAM! Another barrel was lost to the ether. Onward, Mario trod, the slight incline of the steel girder feeling like the slope of the mighty Everest.

And then he heard it. Whether it was the roar of a rolling barrel or the growl of the giant ape, Mario did not know. What he had no doubts about whatsoever was that the sound shook him to his very core.

YOU MUST CHOOSE!

Would you rather...

HAVE A HEAD THAT REFLECTS LIGHT LIKE A DISCO PARTY BALL

OR

PUFF UP LIKE A BLOWFISH WHEN YOU SENSE DANGER?

Would you rather...

exchange reciprocal blumpkins with John Madden

OR

be wagon-trained by a pack of Oompa-Loompas?

Would you rather...

have an irresistible compulsion to lick your throwing hand's thumb like a quarterback every few seconds

OR

have to have at least one hand on your crotch at all times (that hand doesn't have to belong to you)?

Would you rather...

breathe to the rhythm of "Eine Kleine Nacht Musik" by Mozart

OR

have a harmonica implanted in your nasal passageway?

YOU MUST CHOOSE!

Would you rather...

HAVE SKIN SLIGHTLY
TOO SMALL FOR YOUR BODY

OR

SKIN 3 TIMES TOO BIG
FOR YOUR BODY?

Would you rather...

urinate maple syrup

OR

lactate cottage cheese?

Would you rather have your dreams written and directed by...

Quentin Tarantino *OR* Woody Allen?

Ed Wood *OR* the creators of *The Hills*?

John Hughes *OR* Ron Jeremy?

Would you rather...

drool Drain-O

OR

exhale Raid?

Would you rather...

be nail-filed to death

OR

be corkscrewed to death?

YOU MUST CHOOSE!

Would you rather...

be cooked and hardened into a Shrinky Dink

OR

be placed on a giant Spin Art and be spun to death?

Would you rather...

watch a stripper who visibly suffers from severe arthritis **OR** who is stricken with problem flatulence?

who is 60 pounds overweight **OR** who is hot but dances with a Hitler theme?

with protruding varicose veins **OR** who eerily resembles Tommy Lasorda?

Would you rather be stuck on a desert island with...

the complete works of Jane Austen **OR** a year's worth of *Barely Legal*?

your significant other and an iPod filled with Barry White's most sultry tunes **OR** your significant other and a complete set of *Magic: The Gathering* cards?

a fishing rod **OR** a funhouse mirror, a wig, and some K-Y jelly?

YOU MUST CHOOSE!

Would you rather...

die in an avalanche of croutons

OR

drown in a giant bowl of Campbell's New England clam chowder?

Would you rather...

fight a creature that had the body of a bull and the head of a lion

OR

a creature that had the body of an eagle, the head of a snake, and the hair of Donald Trump?

Would you rather...

be a rodeo clown with a bad leg

OR

Danny Bonaduce's personal assistant?

Would you rather...

your hostage negotiator be Robin Williams

OR

Chad Johnson?

YOU MUST CHOOSE!

Would you rather...

HAVE TO SLEEP EACH NIGHT BETWEEN YOUR MATTRESS AND BOX SPRING

OR

COLLECT LINT AT 10,000 TIMES THE NATURAL RATE?

Would you rather...

have a permanent "Got Milk" mustache

OR

have small holes in your cheeks that allowed fluids to leak through like a strainer?

Would you rather...

be a world-class platform diver but painfully envy elk

OR

be able to summarize things with just the right amount of detail but have a codependent relationship with a Yeti?

Would you rather...

only be able to exit buildings through the window

OR

be limited in wardrobe to conquistador garb?

Would you rather...

wake up each day alternating between before and after weight-loss photos

OR

have foam "You're #1" hands in place of your hands?
Things to consider: maintaining a relationship, having two sets of clothes

YOU MUST CHOOSE!

Would you rather...

In the *Great American Race*, would you rather be partnered with...

Lionel Richie *OR* Nick Nolte?

Lance Armstrong *OR* David Blaine?

Hannity *OR* Colmes?

Green Lantern *OR* Superman?

Would you rather...

only be able to speak using words contained in Air Supply songs
OR Black Sabbath songs?

words from the *Gilligan's Island* theme song *OR* the *Cheers* theme song?

words in the song "Macarena" *OR* "Rico Suave"?

Would you rather...

be mysteriously compelled to say "ARRR" in a pirate's voice, before every sentence you speak

OR

to say "Sheeeyyiiitttt" at the end of every sentence?

YOU MUST CHOOSE!

Would you rather...

cut off the tips of your fingers with a band saw

OR

consume, in one seating, 300 Three Musketeers bars?

Would you rather...

as a child, be reared by Britney Spears

OR

K-Fed?

Things to consider: driving, Popozao lullabies

Would you rather...

have your life scored by John Williams

OR

have the song "Whoomp There It Is" play at 120 decibels whenever you complete a bowel movement?

Things to consider: using public restrooms

Would you rather...

always wear your hair in the style of an '80s big hair band

OR

your pants?

YOU MUST CHOOSE!

Would you rather...

be incapable of differentiating between paper shredders and mailboxes **OR** between water fountains and urinals?

between cottage cheese and shampoo **OR** between cell phones and handguns?

between being tired and being lost **OR** between George Gervin and love?

Would you rather...

be a Boltaur—you have your body's upper half and Manute Bol's lower half

OR

a Rubetar—you have your body's lower half and Ruben Studdard's upper half?

Would you rather...

speak in the voice of a possessed Linda Blair in *The Exorcist* whenever talking to cashiers and retail workers

OR

have "Starbucks Tourettes" where you randomly exclaim Starbucks orders? (for example... "Hi, How are—Double Decaf Iced Mocha Frap!")

YOU MUST CHOOSE!

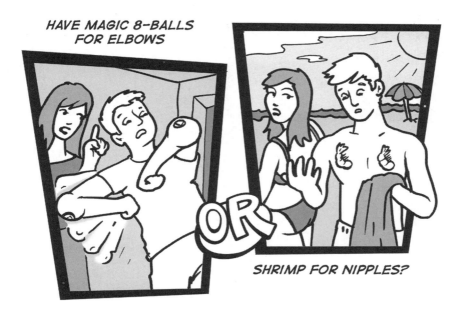

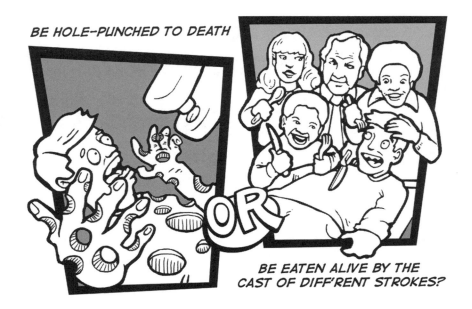

Would you rather...

have a cork back, a comb-over beard, lust after Puss in Boots, have Wes Unseld's shadow, play daily Arkanoid games with Tony Randall, have to register for your wedding at Spencers Gifts, and have basil-scented farts

OR

have butter-soaked skin, a maple scone for an ear, get a five o'clock shadow all over your body, act like Joe Namath when drunk, have a vast coaster collection, have Carl Weathers borrow your pen and never give it back, and have a bulimia that causes you to want to throw up in mail slots?

Would you rather...

have Swiffers for feet

OR

Venetian-blind style eyelids?

YOU MUST CHOOSE!

Chapter Nineteen

Other Mentally Ill-ustrators

Except where noted, up to this point, all of the illustrations for this book have been drawn by the lovely and demented Jason Rooney. Jason emerged as the champion of an exhaustive *American Idol*-like contest to find an illustrator for *Would You Rather...?* However, there were other talented artists as well whose takes on the *WYR* dilemmas ranged from whimsical to the existential and angst-ridden. The following are some of our favorite illustrations.

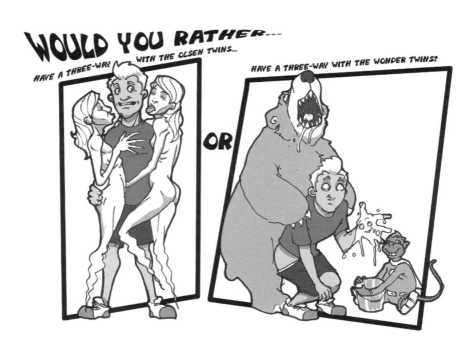

by Jason Brown

by Jason Mayoh

WOULD YOU RATHER
HAVE WORMS FOR EYELASHES OR CORDUROY SKIN?

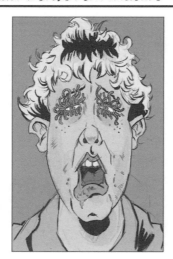

by Jason Mayoh

by Jason Mayoh

Would You Rather

...take a power drill in the Adam's apple

OR

...fill your pants with raw meat
and kick a pit bull in the side?

...have lit candlewicks for hair

OR

...asparagus for fingers?

by Matt Curtis

Would You Rather

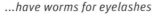
...have worms for eyelashes

OR

...Corduroy skin?

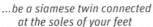
...be a siamese twin connected
at the soles of your feet

OR

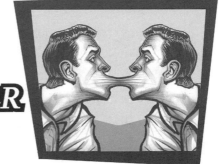
...at the lips?

by Matt Curtis

by Dan Thompson

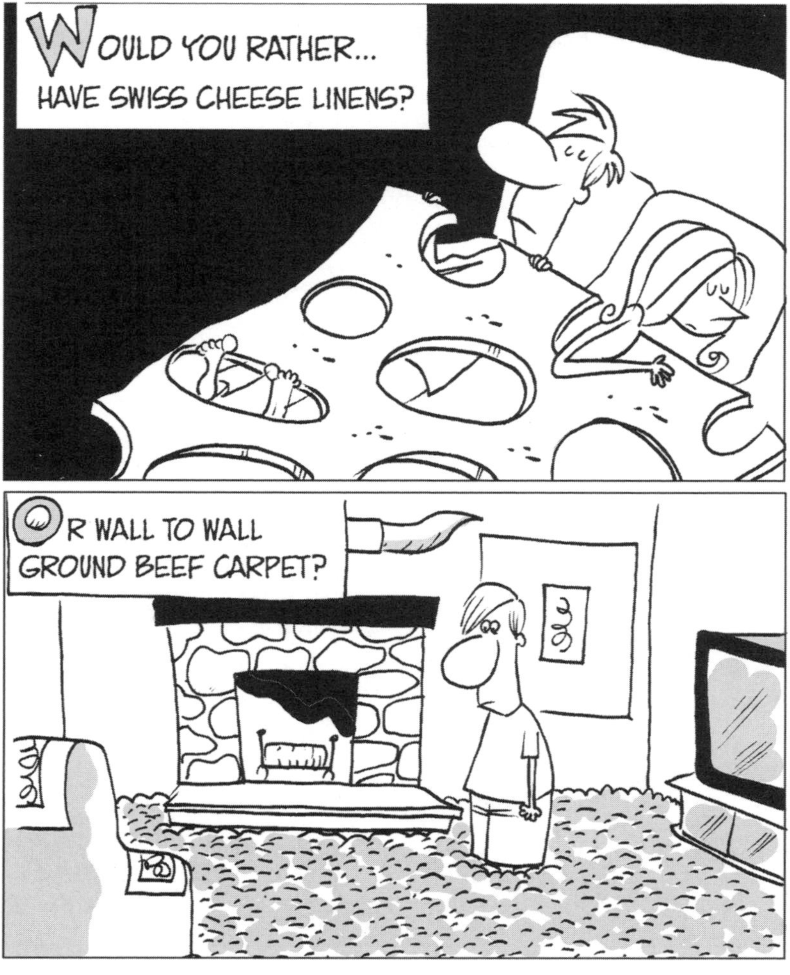

by Dan Thompson

by Dan Thompson

by Erik Craddock

Would you rather...?

TAKE A POWER DRILL IN
THE ADAM'S APPLE...

...OR FILL YOUR PANTS WITH
RAW MEAT AND KICK A PIT
BULL IN THE SIDE?

by Erik Craddock

Would you rather...?

HAVE YOUR CELL PHONE
SET ON AIRHORN...

...OR TASER?

by Erik Craddock

Would you rather...

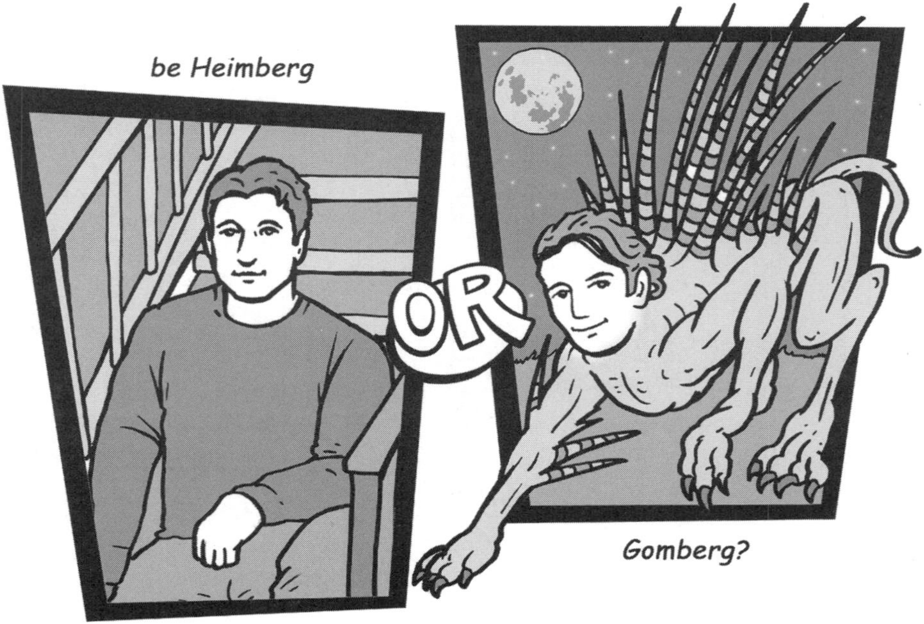

About the Authors

Justin Heimberg is the author of all kinds of comedy books for all ages including the best-selling *Would You Rather...?* series (over 400,000 books in print). He is a professional screenwriter who has worked with studios such as Disney, Paramount, and Universal and collaborated with talent such as Jerry Bruckheimer and Jason Alexander. Justin has served as a humor writer/contributing editor for magazines including *Details*, *Esquire*, and *MAD*. With David Gomberg, Justin runs Seven Footer Entertainment, an entertainment company specializing in short and funny creative projects and services. A trained improvisational performer, Justin is the creator of the Award-winning Documentary at Improv Olympic. He lives in the Washington D.C. area. Justinheimberg.com.

David Gomberg is an outsider from planes dominated by evil forces. He resembles a furless monkey crossed with a sickly dog, and has a vaguely human-like face. He is grey in color, with the slightest hints of violet. For no apparent reason, his shoulders jut sharply up in ugly extremeties. Growing along his back and from his front legs, are sharp quills. Gomberg spends the time when he isn't hunting, howling. The eerie, resonating noise causes anyone who hears it for an extensive amount of time to go mad. When hunting, Gomberg travels in packs. He attacks prey by charging in, then leaving again, then charging back, and so on. He causes damage in this method by thrashing about and scratching prey with his sharp quills. Occasionally, Gomberg might also bellow a particularly focused howl in the victim's face. Gomberg, strangely, is sometimes valued and trained as a mounted steed.

About the Deity

The ringmaster/MC/overlord of the *Would You Rather...?* empire is "the Deity." Psychologically and physically a cross between Charles Manson and Gabe Kaplan, the Deity is the one responsible for creating and presenting the WYR dilemmas. It is the Deity who asks **"Would you rather... watch a porno movie with your parents or a porno movie starring your parents?"** And it is the Deity who orders, without exception, that you must choose. No one knows exactly why he does this; suffice to say, it's for reasons beyond your understanding. The Deity communicates with you not through speech, nor telepathy, but rather through several sharp blows to the stomach that vary in power and location. Nearly omnipotent, often ruthless, and obsessed with former NBA seven-footers, the Deity is a random idea generator with a peculiar predilection for intervening in your life in the strangest ways.

About *Would You Rather...?*® Books:

Us guys, the authors of the *Would You Rather...?* books, believe that the great joys in life are the times spent hanging out with your friends, laughing. Our books aim to facilitate that. They are Socially Interactive Humor Books. SIHB's. Damnit, that acronym sucks! Let's try again... Socially Interactive Games & Humor SIGH... exactly the opposite of what we are looking for in an abbreviation. Son of a bitch. Alright look, these books make you think in interesting ways and talk to your friends, and laugh and be funny. They are, and they make you, imaginative and irreverent. Lots of bang for your buck (and vice versa.) *WYR* books provide 3-300 hrs of entertainment depending on how painfully retarded your reading pace is. So take these books, hang out with your friends, and have a good time.

About the Font

This font, Scala Sans, is an asshole, virtually impossible to work with. Total diva, always wanting to be made bold and enlarged. What prick, seriously! Kept talking shit about Times New Roman and Courier as sell-outs, and spreading false rumors that Century Gothic was gay. We would constantly hear shouting from its trailer, and find demure female fonts like *Brush Script* running out alarmed, exclaiming "That is disgusting!" So Scala Sans font, up yours! You suck!

Other *Would You Rather...?*® Books:

Would You Rather...?: Love & Sex asks you to ponder such questions as:

- **Would you rather...** orgasm once every ten years *OR* once every ten seconds?

- **Would you rather...** have to have sex in the same position every night *OR* have to have sex in a different position every night (you can never repeat)?

- **Would you rather...** have breast implants made of Nerf® *OR* Play-Doh®?

- **Would you rather...** have sex with the new Daisy Duke (Jessica Simpson) *OR* classic Daisy Duke (Catherine Bach)?

- **Would you rather...** vicariously experience all orgasms that occur in your zip code *OR* during sex, have the Microsoft paper clip help icon appear with sex tips?

Would You Rather...?: Love & Sex can be read alone or played together as a game. Laugh-out-loud funny, uniquely imaginative, and deceptively thought-provoking, *Would You Rather...?: Love & Sex* is simultaneously the authors' most mature and immature work yet!

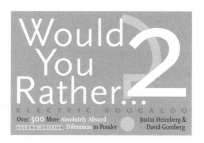

Would You Rather...?® 2: Electric Boogaloo
Another collection of over three hundred
absurd alternatives and demented dilemmas.
Filled with wacky wit, irreverent humor and
twisted pop-culture references.

Would You Rather...?: Pop Culture Edition
A brand new collection of deranged
dilemmas and preposterous predicaments,
featuring celebrities and trends from popular
culture. Ponder and debate questions like:
Would you rather... be machine-gunned to
death with Lite-Brite pegs *OR* be
assassinated by Cabbage Patch Dolls?

Would You Rather...?'s What Would You Be?
Stretch your metaphor muscles along with
your imagination as you answer and discuss
thought/humor-provoking questions like:
If you were a Smurf, which one would you
be? What if you were a type of dog?
A road sign? A Beatle? A nonsense sound?

Would You Rather...? for Kids

The first book in the series written and designed for kids ages 8 and older, *Would You Rather...? for Kids* features hundreds of devilish dilemmas and imaginative illustrations! Kids will crack up as they ponder questions such as:
Would you rather... have a tape-dispensing mouth *OR* a bottle-opening nostril?

Would You Rather...?: Illustrated

Tired of having to visualize these dilemmas yourself? No need any more with this book of masterfully illustrated *Would You Rather...?* dilemmas. Now you can see what it looks like to be attacked by hundreds of Pilsbury Doughboys, get hole-punched to death, sweat cheese, or have pubic hair that grows an inch every second. A feast for the eyes and imagination, *Would You Rather...?: Illustrated* gives Salvador Dali a run for his money.

Would You Rather...?'s What's Your Price?
Would you punch your grandmother in the stomach as hard as you can for $500,000? There are no wrong answers but hundreds of "wrong" questions in this irresistibly irreverent book.

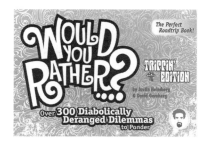

Would You Rather...? Trippin' Edition
Take a trip, in your car or in your mind, as you ponder the truly bizarre. *Would You Rather...? Trippin' Edition* is a brand new batch of laugh-out-loud funny and deceptively thought-provoking quirky quandaries. Filled with pop culture references, this ice-breaking, party-pleasing, time-killing, road-tripping, hilarious socially interactive book is filled with all-new travel games. Perfect for the car, dorm room, train, monorail, zeppelin, jail cell, toilet, or jail cell toilet.

More Books by Seven Footer Press

MindF✲cks

From the authors of the *Would You Rather...?* books, comes *MindF✲cks*, an instructional primer on creating mass confusion with simple acts of senselessness. Taking aim at everyday situations and locations ranging from elevators to driving tests to the office, *MindF✲cks* offers over 800 ways to amuse yourself by bemusing others.

The Official Movie Plot Generator

"A Coffee Table Masterpiece" - *Newsweek*.

The Official Movie Plot Generator is a unique and interactive humor book that offers 27,000 hilarious movie plot possibilities you create, spanning every genre of cinema from feel-good family fun to hard-boiled crime drama to soft-core

pornography. Just flip the book's ninety tabs until you find a plot combination you like. For movie fans or anyone who likes to laugh a lot with little effort, *The Official Movie Plot Generator* is a perfect gift and an irresistible, offbeat diversion.

Pornification

"For every legit movie, there exists (at least theoretically), a porn version of that movie." *Pornification* includes over 500 "pornified" titles, along with hysterical quizzes, games and challenges. There's something for everyone, from *Cold Mountin'* to *The Fast and Bicurious* to *Malcolm XXX*, so open up and enjoy!

The Yo Momma Vocabulary Builder

Increasing word power sounds like one of those dreary chores best palmed off on somebody else. *The Yo Momma Vocabulary Builder*, the first in Seven Footer's series of irreverent, educational books, makes the activity not only endurable but irresistible. The authors use classic dissing and one-upsmanship to slyly introduce a wide range of words.

Available at www.wouldyourather.com

Coming Soon:
Other *Would You Rather...?*® books
by the authors

Wouldn't You Rather...?: Over 200 Pointed Questions to Answer
Sample question: **Wouldn't you rather...** go to the beach than the mountains?
Things to consider: I mean, really, it's obvious, isn't it? Sun? Surf? Jeez!

Would You Rather...? Australia
Sample question: **Would you rather...** take a walkabout with bunyips and yowies
in nothing but your stubbies *OR* get in a barney with a fair-dinkum yobbo?
Things to consider: chooks, dunny-buggies

Would You Rather...? Mormon Edition
Sample question: **Would you rather...** marry a Mormon spouse, thereby sealing
your eternal place in the Celestial Kingdom *OR* be allowed to drink coffee?

Got Your Own Question?

Go to www.wouldyourather.com to submit your questions and share them with others. Read and debate thousands of other dilemmas submitted by the authors and users.

www.wouldyourather.com

Featuring:
- New Questions

- Humor books and games

- Other *Would You Rather...?* products

- Contests

- Comedy videos, e-cards, animations and more!